HOMECOMING

HOMECOMING

A "White" Man's Journey through Harlem to Jerusalem

Curtiss Paul DeYoung

Jezi Press
Minneapolis

HOMECOMING
A "White" Man's Journey through Harlem to Jerusalem

Unless noted otherwise all quotes from the Bible are from the New Revised Standard Version. Qur'an quotations are from M.A.S. Abdel Haleem, *The Qur'an*, (New York: Oxford University Press, 2004).

Cover image: The photo on the front cover was taken with my camera by Eliyahu McLean while we were at the mystical canyon in Tekoa /Teqoa in the West Bank of Palestine (see chapter 7). For me it visually represents the mystery of God's invitation to take the path leading to homecoming.

Interior: The photo introducing part 1 was taken by David Baird in the fall of 1982. I was just shy of twenty-five years. David was my roommate in college and at the time was a journalist. The photo introducing part 2 was taken by my daughter, Rachel DeYoung, in the summer of 2006. I was almost forty-nine years old. I bought the galabya and the kufi cap on the Nile River in Egypt. Both photos have a similar story. The Baird photo was shot to appear like it was taken in New York City. It was actually shot in Anderson, Indiana, after I left New York. The second photo appears to be taken in the Middle East. It was taken a few months after my visit to Egypt and Palestine in Minneapolis, Minnesota. These photos symbolize for me that while I returned to familiar places I was a different person. Transformation had occurred.

Library of Congress Cataloging-in-Publication Data
ISBN 978-0-692-00227-8

CONTENTS

Prologue: Tears at a Homecoming   1

    PART ONE—HARLEM TO ROXBURY   9
    The Complexities of Race and Identity in America

1.   Glimpses of My Humanity in Harlem   11
2.   Linked to a Lineage of Mentors   29
3.   A "White" Malcolm X   43
4.   Taco Bell Lutheran   59

Interlude One: Roots in Roxbury   78

    PART TWO—JOHANNESBURG TO JERUSALEM   85
    The Intersection of Global Cultures and Religious Faiths

5.   A Global Faith   87
6.   The Jesus Was Black Tour   99
7.   The Peace of Jerusalem   113

Interlude Two: Roots in Africa   129

Epilogue: The Homecoming Dance   133
Afterword: The Journey Continues   143
Acknowledgments   147
Notes   149

PROLOGUE

Tears at a Homecoming

Something happened to me the first time I visited the continent of Africa. It is difficult to find
the words to articulate this unanticipated experience. In the
midst of a leadership conference for Christian youth workers
in 2000, where I was a workshop presenter, I was informed
that I would be the guest preacher at a service the following
evening for all of the participants. Even with only twenty-
four hours to prepare, I was pleased and excited by this unexpected opportunity.

I arrived that evening ready to preach. After being introduced, I walked onto the stage and approached the micro-
phone. Only no words came out of my mouth. I could not
speak. I was completely overwhelmed by emotion. Instead of
words I had only tears. Some of the youth workers and young
people in attendance laughed nervously. Most waited quietly
for me to begin speaking. I realized that an explanation was
expected and needed. It is not every day that a grown man
and guest speaker from the United States stands before an
African crowd and cries for no apparent reason. In an emo-
tion-laden voice I said, "I feel like I have come home." I then
struggled to regain my composure and preached my sermon.

The conference was held near Johannesburg, South Africa.
The next day at breakfast, a few of the white leaders invited
me to join them at their table. They asked me to talk about

1

what I meant when I said, "I feel like I have come home." They asked if it was related to my interracial marriage to an African American woman. I was not quite sure where this conversation was headed. I responded by saying that I did not know what had provoked my statement. I added that the phrase might have been theological. I had spent much time writing and speaking about the biblical material in Genesis that speaks of humanity's origins in an Eden that stretched from Africa to Asia. So perhaps my arrival on African soil for the first time was a theological homecoming.

I could not articulate what prompted the emotions or the words about homecoming. I certainly was moved by the worship that emerged from a multicultural crowd reflecting the rainbow of people in South Africa. Among those assembled were black indigenous Africans from many cultures and languages, Coloureds (people of mixed-race descent), Indians (originating from the continent of India), and both Afrikaans- and English-speaking whites. People from other nations of Africa were also in attendance. Beautiful indigenous African musical forms integrated with elements of Europe and even traces of gospel music from the United States to create an exhilarating worship celebration.

It was a powerful and amazing experience to worship God in such a diverse setting. The worship team effectively blended multiple languages and diverse cultural musical styles in ways that I have not experienced in the United States. Songs were sung from different cultures and languages. Many of these songs, no matter what their original language, included verses in two or three additional languages (among the eleven official languages of South Africa). The participants also added various dance moves from the many cultures represented. As the musicians and singers shifted from one language, cultural sound, and rhythm to the next, simultaneously the worship participants would change to a culturally related dance expression.

The diversity in language, culture, style, and expression was dramatic, inspirational, and mesmerizing.

Just before I stepped up on the platform to preach, I reflected on my pastor and mentor Samuel Hines, the Jamaican-born expository preacher who had proclaimed a message of reconciliation so many times in South Africa during the days of apartheid. And here I was five years after his death, his son in ministry, continuing his legacy of preaching reconciliation but now in a liberated South Africa. Perhaps my depth of feeling came from dreaming for so long of visiting South Africa and now experiencing a dream come true. I am sure the emotions also included missing my wife Karen. I was across the world from the woman I loved. And I so wished that she had been there with me.

I had not considered my visit to Africa as a homecoming experience. This thought often occurs to African Americans when they visit the continent of Africa. Many persons of African descent from the United States feel as though Mother Africa is beckoning them, as her children, to come home. It seemed to me that those words—"I feel like I have come home"—were just an impromptu response to why I had been overcome by emotion.

Upon further reflection, I realized that the intense emotions driving my words came from very deep within me. I now believe that some sort of primal feeling emerged. I had a brief experience of homecoming. In that instant I was no longer locked into any of the identity definers we wear in society based on race, ethnicity, gender, social class, and the like. I was at home with myself. I was a child of God, created in the image of God. Truthfully, I cannot say with certainty what prompted this experience. All I know is that God touched me that night in a very profound way. For a brief moment, I stood spiritually naked and unashamed before the God who created me. Even now I still experience the emotions afresh when I speak of the event.

When we are born we arrive as a simple human being. But the second we take our first breath, society busily assigns meaning to our personhood. Our physical appearance is assessed using social norms that define our future according to skin color, beauty standards, physical size, and the like. Our biological sex leads to socialization into certain expected gender roles. The economic class or social status of our parents dramatically affects our opportunities in society. Our family's religion, culture, and language are viewed as either advantages or disadvantages in the nation of our birth. The nation where we are born also determines our place in the larger world. Certainly, if we are born with any physical, mental, or psychological challenges we are marked in society by this feature.

When I say that I felt spiritually naked and unashamed before God during that brief moment in South Africa, I am claiming that for a few seconds I seemed to know myself in the manner that I arrived rather than in the identity defined for me by society. I felt stripped clean of socially constructed meaning and free to encounter divine worth. It was a homecoming with my humanity—stamped with the imprint of God's divine image. Perhaps this is what is meant in the third chapter of the Gospel of John when Jesus referred to being born again or born from above (3:3-8). To be born again is to rediscover and reclaim God's original design for our identity. At some very deep level, I believe we all desire such a homecoming.

Aspects of my identity have been shaped by the particularities of how society constructs or defines my reality—white, male, Christian, Protestant, Church of God, middle-class, educated, able-bodied, six feet tall, left-handed, heterosexual, English speaking, and a citizen of the United States of America. My early upbringing would appear to most as predicting a monocultural, isolated, think-alike, look-alike existence. I am ethnically Dutch and English—a nice white Anglo Saxon Protestant (WASP). I was born in an area affectionately known as "Amish Country." I lived in rural towns and suburbs named LaGrange, Dowagiac, Pratt, Plainwell, Portage, and Otsego. I attended a predominately white, middle-class Christian college located in a region where the Ku Klux Klan was still active. I was on track to live a comfortable, one-dimensional life that was in line with my white, middle-class status.

But that is not what happened. Because of periodic glimpses of the beauty of our common humanity juxtaposed with troubling observations of the ugliness of injustice, a transformation took place. As a result, much of my life as an adult has been in multicultural urban settings in such places as New York City, Minneapolis, and Washington, DC. People often ask how I became the person I am now. What happened to change the course of my life? How could I be born in rural Indiana and later work in large cities? How could I come from a monocultural family of origin and thrive in multicultural settings? I believe this occurred because somehow in the midst of isolated circumstances I was granted a number of opportunities to peer through life's experiential windows and see fresh perspectives.

Something grander and more comprehensive has been at work in my life's journey. My journey has been informed by powerfully instructive interludes, experiences that integrated many other distinctive paths therefore creating a more universal human trek. In the pages that follow, I describe these transforming interruptions, these epiphany moments, that occurred in places like New York City and Washington, DC, as well as in Salzburg, Austria, in various cities in South Africa, and in Jerusalem.

I have understood my life journey in various ways through the years. At times I have seen it through a geographic lens that led from birth in rural Indiana, upbringing in suburban Michigan, to working in our nation's cities. I have also defined my life's direction and vocational calling as reconciliation in urban multicultural settings. Over the past few years I have come to believe that my journey has really been about rediscovering the essence of what it means to be human—created in the image of God.

This book is about rediscovering and embracing our full humanity. I share and reflect on autobiographical anecdotes and encounters from my own life that have provided me with glimpses into the notion of what it means to embrace my humanity and that of my fellow residents on planet Earth. I am more interested in divine meaning than human chronology, so I do not always tell my story in a linear fashion. I try to be transparent and vulnerable in the telling. I want this to be a complete work in the sense that it reveals the delightful surprises and joys found on the journey, as well as the blemishes and sinfulness discovered in the mirror of self-reflection. I also seek to discover the limitations in apparent privilege and to discuss the real pain of struggle. Certain episodes may push you beyond your comfort zones. I am familiar with that experience. Portions of my story are about those moments in my life when I was stretched in so many ways.

This book recounts my story. This is how I understand my story after a half century of living. In the next ten, twenty, or thirty years my journey certainly will take some unexpected turns, and I may need to retell this story with fresh wisdom and greater nuance. You may not always agree with my perspective, but this represents my viewpoint and interpretation at age fifty. This is not the story of my wife, children, family, friends, mentors, or colleagues. I do not try to tell their stories. I speak of them as they connect with my narrative and hopefully only in ways that bring honor to the impact they have had on my life. I invite you to reflect on your own homecoming journey as you engage with my adventure—only then will I have achieved my purpose in publishing this book.

Howard Thurman wrote that "life is regarded as a pilgrimage, a sojourn, while the true home of the spirit is beyond the vicissitudes of life with God!"[1] The writer of the Hebrews proclaimed, "All of these died in faith without having received the promises, but from a distance they saw and greeted them. They confessed that they were strangers and foreigners on the earth, for people who speak in this way make it clear that they are seeking a homeland…they desire a better country, that is, a heavenly one. Therefore God is not ashamed to be called their God; indeed, he has prepared a city for them" (11:13-14, 16). The author of Hebrews anticipated that same "true home of the spirit" that Howard Thurman later saw "beyond the vicissitudes of life." A heavenly homeland is envisioned as our final destination. We catch glimpses of it in our earthly journey. We hear echoes of the eternal. We taste its sweetness. We smell its fresh aroma. I am far from arriving at the journey's end. So "from a distance" I offer some insights gained that add to our anticipation of homecoming.

Part One
Harlem to Roxbury
The Complexities of Race and Identity in America

❋

The history of the Americas has been shaped by the collisions of empires and cultures. As a result, America's peoples and societies have been stripped of much of their culture and then racialized into a hierarchy of worth. The journey of identity formation has been a complicated affair. My own journey through the labyrinth of self-understanding has been deeply affected, at least since 1630, by these multiple clashes first in British Colonial America and then in the United States of America.

The internal voice inviting me to embrace the fullness of my humanity grew louder as I traveled through New York City, especially Harlem, and Washington, DC, then on to Minneapolis. Along the way, I interacted with a wide range of people. I was shaped by these encounters. The deep hunger for a homecoming, with all of what makes me a human being created in the image of God, led me to journey through the complexities of race and identity in America. The path took me through Harlem in New York City and back in time to Roxbury, Massachusetts.

CHAPTER ONE

Glimpses of My Humanity in Harlem

During my junior year at Anderson College (now University) in 1979, I joined the school's campus pastor, Donald Collins, and a small group of students on a trip to New York City to learn about life in large cities. We visited churches, social service agencies, night court, and some of the tourist sights. For the first time in my life, I closely observed poverty and social injustice. I glimpsed a side of life in the United States that I had rarely noticed before. I was troubled by the degree of poverty I witnessed in the richest country in the world. Walking through the South Bronx in the late 1970s was like exploring a bombed out war zone. Many city blocks were filled with dilapidated apartment buildings. Other blocks contained only the rubble of former buildings. I remember seeing a small child playing with an old tire in an abandoned lot and wondered, "Where are the playgrounds?" I also met recovering heroin addicts who rolled up their sleeves to reveal needle marks and abused veins.

Seeing the effects of poverty firsthand, I knew that I must find a way to respond to what I had witnessed and experienced in New York City. My direction in life was transformed at the intersection of an encounter with the reality of life in the city and a divine epiphany. The words of Jesus came to mind, "To whom much is given, much is expected." Or as the New International Version of the Bible states: "From everyone who has been given much, much more will be demanded" (Luke

12:48). I had been granted an experience—a new way of seeing. Now my life was marked with the divine expectation that I would somehow respond to this growing awareness.

After graduating from college in 1980, I did not immediately pursue this calling. I accepted a position as a youth pastor in a small Michigan town with a population of about five-thousand people. I had decided that I needed to pay my college bills rather than move directly toward city ministry. I was miserable in my new position. I did not feel the joy that comes from being in the center of God's will. I eventually decided that I needed to get back on the course that I felt God was directing me to pursue. While visiting New York in 1979, I had visited a runaway youth shelter called Covenant House run by a Franciscan priest. So I applied and was accepted to serve in a one-year Peace Corps–type position.

After a one-year stint as small town youth pastor, I moved to New York City in 1981 to live and work with the runaway and homeless youth that congregated in the Times Square section of the nation's largest city. This was the early 1980s, and Times Square was the center of the sex industry in the United States. There were over 150 sex-related businesses in the ten-block region called Times Square. It was the center of a North American market that had four times as many adult bookstores and peep shows as McDonald's fast food restaurants. The profits of the sex industry reportedly exceeded that of the record and movie industry combined. Times Square had a flourishing drug trade and was a magnet for homeless adults, teenagers, and children. When the taxicab driver stopped in Times Square, where I would live and work for the next year, he asked if I was sure this was the right place. I was unprepared for the challenges that lay ahead and naive to the reality of street life. The taxi driver was right to be concerned. I was sure only that I believed I was doing God's will. This was the beginning of my response to the divine expectation.

I made a yearlong commitment to work at Under 21—a shelter for homeless youth in Times Square run by Covenant House. For several months I lived in a room that overlooked the corner of Eighth Avenue and Forty-Fourth Street. Every night I could peer out my window and observe a sordid world where people were stripped of their dignity and sense of humanity through prostitution. As I traversed the streets of Times Square, I looked into eyes that betrayed pain. I walked into roach- and rat-infested dwellings. I was offered drugs and sex. I saw a man lying on the street in a pool of blood. Life was harsh. Times Square was also a place where the very rich and the very poor crossed paths. I remember seeing a woman wearing a mink coat step out of a limousine and walk past a homeless man searching through a garbage container. She entered a Broadway theatre while he consumed the half-eaten piece of pizza he had found.

Serving in New York City put real faces on my romantic notions of "working with the poor." I often felt hopeless in the midst of the complex systemic problems of urban life. I was helpless listening to the cries of women, men, youth, children, and babies being crushed by the system. I learned quickly that the young people who found their way to the Under 21 shelter often were not valued by families, friends, and society at large. They lived at the margins, sleeping on the streets or in homeless shelters because they did not count.

In each person I met, I tried to see something that validated her or his humanity. I challenged myself to find something good in each young person that crossed my path at the Under 21 shelter. Some of the youth made that more difficult due to bravado, posture, or the tragedy of their circumstances. I met teenage mothers with multiple children, young people pushed out of their homes by their parents because of bad behavior who now needed shelter. One fifteen-year-old child had gone to school in the morning and returned home that same afternoon to learn that his family had moved and left no forwarding address. Many young people were fleeing situations of physical and sexual abuse.

Sometimes it was difficult not to determine the worth of these youth by their tragedies, situations, choices, or appearances. Many were victimized by their circumstances. It was easy to disregard them as helpless victims without hope. It was tempting to define some of these young women and men simply as drug addicts, prostitutes, delinquents, gangsters, or worse, children of the devil. But I always tried to remember that the young people I encountered had value because they were children of God and, therefore, not without hope.

The move to New York City was a dramatic change for me. I left a monocultural, monolingual setting for a place that was home to people from a multiplicity of cultures, races, and languages. In Michigan I had served a congregation of my own Protestant denomination. In New York I lived as a part of the Covenant House Faith Community, a Franciscan Roman Catholic lay community where I attended Mass everyday and participated in a prayer life that included chanting the Psalms. I moved from a leisurely-paced small town to a fast-paced big city. The magnitude of the change that occurred in my life was illustrated by an event that occurred about a month after I arrived in New York. I attended a Simon and Garfunkel reunion concert held in Central Park. Over five hundred thousand people attended the event. In a month's time I had transitioned from living in a town of five thousand people to attending a concert where over half a million people assembled.

I felt completely out of my comfort zone as I worked with homeless youth, walked the streets of New York City, and attended Catholic Mass. I was lonely and longing for something or someone familiar. So after living in the city for a few months, and visiting many of the famous churches, I decided to visit a congregation of my own denomination. I was being stretched in so many ways by the New York City experience. I surmised that if I could just enjoy an hour or two with people who looked like me, believed like me, and worshiped like me, I could better maintain the rest of my life. I consulted a list of Church of God congregations to discover which was closest to where I lived in Times Square and big enough that I could slip in to check it out without drawing attention to myself. The one that seemed to match that description best was the Congregational Church of God at 154th Street and Amsterdam Avenue.

I entered the subway station on a quiet Sunday morning. The A train pulled up, I stepped into the train and rode to 145th Street. There I transferred to the AA local and rode that subway car to the stop at 155th Street. I walked a few blocks to my destination and opened the front door of the church building. It quickly became apparent to me that the membership of the congregation was entirely African American. I was unaware that 154th Street and Amsterdam Avenue is in the northern section of Harlem, a cultural Mecca for African Americans. So much for finding a comfort zone!

An usher greeted me by asking, "May I help you?" While the usher's question was presented in a warm and friendly manner, it belied the fact that someone of my complexion had not walked through those doors in quite some time. I mentioned that I was a member of the Church of God and a recent graduate from Anderson College, a Church of God–affiliated school in Anderson, Indiana. I was then ushered into the sanctuary. Some seasoned members of the congregation beckoned me to sit next to them.

The worship service soon began, although the pastor was nowhere in sight. (I would learn later that this was called the devotional service and was led by lay members.) A few minutes later a gentleman stepped out from a door behind the platform and motioned in my direction for me to step forward. I looked around and realized that he was gesturing at me. So I left my seat and followed him through the door. He introduced himself as the chair of the board. He informed me that the pastor wanted to meet me. I was then directed into the office of Pastor Levorn Aaron. Apparently, the news of my arrival had quickly made its way to the pastor's office.

Dr. Aaron greeted me warmly. He noted that he had been informed that I was a member of the Church of God and had attended Anderson College. Then he asked me, "Do you know my boy, Jim?" I was bewildered by the question, thinking that perhaps his son had attended the college in Anderson. Pastor Aaron again asked, "Do you know my boy, Jim?" Then noticing my obvious lack of comprehension, he added, "Jim Massey." In his colloquial manner he was asking if I knew his friend Dr. James Earl Massey—the esteemed biblical scholar and preacher in residence at Anderson College and School of Theology. (As students, we never would have considered calling Dr. Massey "Jim.") I assured Pastor Aaron that I indeed did know his friend "Jim" Massey and had taken several courses from him. To have studied at the feet of Dr. James Earl Massey was all the reference I needed.

Pastor Aaron next asked if I was a minister. I responded that I was not yet ordained but had been licensed as a minister while serving as a youth pastor in Michigan. He then opened his calendar of church activities and asked if I could preach at the congregation on the Sunday morning two weeks following. I was stunned. I had only been in the church building for a matter of minutes, and now I was being asked to preach. Of course I said yes. And thus began a wonderful year that would transform my life. I preached for a Sunday morning service nearly once a month during the year I lived in New York City. Actually, Rev. Aaron and the congregation taught me how to preach. I learned to slow my pace and treat preaching as a dialogue rather than a monologue. The congregation encouraged and supported me with their verbal responses.

Dr. Aaron designated me his associate minister—"Minister Curt"—and trained me in urban ministry as his apprentice. Apprenticeship is the traditional method of leadership development in many urban congregations and particularly among African Americans. Aaron was a seasoned pastor who yearned for the opportunity to equip a young minister in the ways of urban church life. There were no other young ministers in the congregation. That first Sunday when I was escorted into the pastor's office, Levorn Aaron did not exclusively see a white man. Oh, I am sure that he noticed my whiteness. But what he observed was a young minister who was in need of training for urban ministry. And he was eager to offer an apprenticeship.

The experience in this Harlem congregation also provided me with the opportunity to live and worship in an African American setting. Many of my stereotypes were corrected. My one-dimensional view of African American life expanded. My definition of the human family broadened. Initially, I was preoccupied with the differences. In my first weeks at the church, I would tell others how excited I was to attend this "black" church with "black" preaching and "black" worship. Pointing out the "blackness" of the experience revealed my own sense of feeling different. Soon the "race" adjectives dropped and I enjoyed attending my church with its powerful preaching and inspiring worship. At the Congregational Church of God, I also learned what it meant to be accepted unconditionally as a human being. Reverend Aaron and the congregation never brought it to my attention that I was "different"—white. I was welcomed simply as a member of the church family, a child of God, a human being.

My experience at Covenant House was also life changing. I worked with runaway and homeless youth from varied backgrounds who seemed foreign to my sensibilities. Poverty became more than a concept. The "poor" had faces and personalities. The "poor" were people. The "poor" were more than the label "poor." Periodically, the actions of those I thought I was serving were a service to me. A teenage girl who had run away from home came into the Under 21 shelter badly beaten. She was ensnared in prostitution and had been assaulted by her pimp. She had been in and out of the shelter up to this point. On this particular visit she asked me if I still prayed. She was aware that those of us in the faith community were people of prayer. I reassured her that I did. Her parents did not want her to return home, assuming that she would have a negative influence on a younger sister. She knelt down in front of me, tied a piece of ribbon on the lace of one of my sneakers, and pleaded with me to pray that she could go home. Although she asked me to pray for her, she honored me in an act that evoked an image of the woman who kissed and anointed Jesus' feet (Luke 7:36-39). The young woman did go home and later enrolled in nursing school. And I remained affirmed by a generous act of humility and grace from a person many would see as "poor."[1]

Life in the Covenant House Faith Community taught me much about the Catholic spiritual and mystical tradition that still enriches me today. I joined other community members in a commitment to three hours of prayer a day in the Franciscan tradition of prayer: morning prayer, Mass, and evening prayer. Covenant House had a unique chapel, the Chapel of the Crucifixion that featured a twenty-four-by-thirty-foot copper relief mural called "Passion on Eighth Avenue." The mural merged the scene of Jesus' crucifixion with life on the streets of New York City. Everyday I sat in that chapel meditating, praying, and worshiping with hopes of integrating my faith and life in New York City. I also experienced Franciscan inspired communal living and commitment to simplicity. The year at Covenant House caused a significant shift in my values. I became less enamored with material things. I gained an appreciation for the importance of community and service. I learned to live a faith that was radical in its acting out of a belief rooted in social justice. I developed a fuller inner life with God. I gained a deep and abiding affection for my Catholic sisters and brothers in Christ. When I later took a course at the Dominican House of Studies in Washington, DC, I was already at home in the culture and ways of Catholicism.

But a particular experience in the Covenant House Faith Community contradicted my experience at the Congregational Church of God in Harlem. At the Harlem church, I was fully embraced and included as a member without reservation in regard to my whiteness. At Covenant House, I was a Protestant in a Catholic community. Everyday during Eucharist at the daily Mass, I was reminded of my difference. All of the Catholic faith community members went forward to receive the bread and the wine. The spiritual director of the faith community had informed me that I should not partake because my view of communion differed from that of Roman Catholics. Out of respect for my Catholic sisters and brothers I remained in my seat. But I was troubled by this practice.

In a community that spoke often of justice and inclusion, I sensed I was being excluded and treated like an outsider. As a Protestant I felt like a second-class citizen. As time passed the experience of not receiving the full gifts of Christian membership weighed heavily on me. I became demoralized. We often sang a song by John B. Foley, "One Bread, One Body," as the Eucharist was served. I did not experience the sense of oneness described in that song during Mass. Some community members noticed my despondency in Mass and sought to encourage me.

In the spirit of the social justice activism I had learned from many in the faith community, I challenged the practice of excluding Protestants from this ritual that I believed pointed

to the unity of the church. Near the end of my stay, I submitted "The Eucharist Proposal" to the governing council of the
Covenant House Faith Community:

> I propose that the Council find a way to make the Eucharist
> available to Covenant Community members, whether they
> are Catholic or Protestant. The Eucharist should be the
> element of unity in a community. It is a time for expressing
> unity with Christ and the community. The Eucharist was
> instituted by the Lord himself and we show our love for
> Christ by remembering him in this act.... This proposal is
> written with concern for the present Community members
> that do not receive the Eucharist and in memory of those
> who have suffered this injustice in the past. I also write this for
> the Catholics in this community who deeply desire to see real
> spiritual unity in this community. The Covenant Community
> should witness that Christians can live together and share the
> Eucharist together despite differences in doctrine. By making
> this proposal a reality, this community would become a
> beacon of hope to a divided church.

The proposal included some process steps for achieving
its sentiments. The Eucharist Proposal eventually found its
way to the founder and president of Covenant House, Father
Bruce Ritter.

My strongly worded proposal dismayed Father Ritter, and
the faith community was divided over how to respond to my
expressed concerns. The governing council called an all-com-
munity meeting. On one side of the room was Father Bruce
Ritter, a fifty-five-year-old, Ph.D.-trained medieval scholar
and president of one of the largest faith-based charities in the
United States, accompanied by community members who felt
that no change was necessary. I sat on the other side of the
room as a twenty-four-year-old, barely trained and not-yet-
ordained Protestant minister, joined by many Catholic community members who believed that the gospel called for a

change in the practice. Although several of us spoke in favor of my proposal, the debate was over before it began. Ritter said that while he appreciated my concerns he had worked too hard to gain the support of the archdiocese and the Vatican. He would not risk alienating Catholic leaders for something like this. The discussion ended with no change being implemented. The founder had spoken.

Immediately after the meeting, Father Ritter took me aside and asked why I had written the letter. Why had I used terms like "injustice"? He informed me that I was not the first Protestant community member to raise the issue. The letter had caused him to relive prior painful encounters. I responded that what I wrote was what I believed and felt regarding the situation. It was clear that Fr. Ritter's respect for me increased because I had stood up for what I believed—and I felt some personal peace that I had pressed the issue as far as possible. Yet nothing had changed at Covenant House. Protestants were still not encouraged to approach the Eucharistic table in the Covenant House Faith Community.

As I reread the Eucharist Proposal over twenty-five years later, I detect some arrogance and immaturity in my presentation. Were I writing it today, I would express more humility and finesse. I also recall the internal struggle that produced the proposal. I hear the cry to be recognized as equal—a full member of the community. And I admire the passion for justice and reconciliation that caused me to pen the proposal. I pray that I will never lose this courageous fervor.

❊❊❊

What I experienced and learned while living in New York City was not apparent to me until I had ample opportunity to reflect on it in the years since. We often view ourselves through the lens of social norms or expectations. We usually are focused on a sub-identity. That is often how people define

us, identify us, and interact with us. Sometimes we find meaning from our various sub-identities. We are a mother, father,
son, daughter, or grandparent. Or we think of our self-worth
in terms of our job or particular talents. Some folks make
their physical appearance the center of their identity, which
may require surgery to maintain as one ages. Of course our
race, gender, culture, and economic status can become ways
for propping up our sense of self. Seldom do we actually experience ourselves or define ourselves from our core identity as
human beings. Howard Thurman wrote regarding racism that
"the burden of being black and the burden of being white is
so heavy that it is rare in our society to experience oneself as
a human being."[2]

Our sub-identities are not bad in themselves. They are
part of who we are. When particular aspects of our identity
are devalued in society, we certainly need to reaffirm our self-
worth. But sub-identities at their best are still one-dimensional
views of our multifaceted humanness. They are part of a much
larger whole. In reality these sub-identities are not the essence
of who we really are as human beings. The core of our identity
is the divine imprint that reminds us we are children of God.

I was embraced by the members of the Congregational
Church of God as a child of God. They viewed me as a person, a human being. I was not reduced to social identifiers. I
was not kept at arms length or treated differently because I was
white. As this community of faith in Harlem reflected back to
me total acceptance, I glimpsed my essence as a human being.
What a life-giving moment! Over time I came to receive this
unconditional acceptance—a rare experience in a society that
emphasizes one's value relative to a worldly point of view. I
rested fully in their embrace.

At the same time, as I was being embraced for my essence
as a child of God in Harlem, I also felt restricted and not fully
included because of my sub-identity as a Protestant. Despite

the best efforts of many caring and concerned individuals in the Covenant House Faith Community, they could not reverse the reality that I was not Roman Catholic and therefore could not approach the communion table. My experience was small compared to the personal assaults of sexism, racism, or classism, but I felt devalued nonetheless.

A woman I once encountered at an urban housing project in Kansas City, Kansas, articulated well the frustration of rejection. She had learned a few days earlier that her home might be demolished in the name of urban renewal. Residents of the housing project met to voice displeasure at the thought of the housing authority bulldozing their neighborhood. I was invited to offer a word of support. I spoke of how encouraged I was by the evidence of a strong desire to save their homes. I suggested that if they could organize and present their concerns as a group, they would have a better chance at attracting the attention of those in power making the decision. After I finished my remarks, this woman rose to respond. She had a look that betrayed weariness, yet at the same time revealed a strange mix of resoluteness, confusion, and anger. She proceeded to ask a most provocative question: "Why shouldn't the voice of one person count? Why will people listen only when there are many? Every person's voice should count!"

I am still haunted by the woman's query: "Why shouldn't the voice of one person count?" The question challenges our willingness as a society to place equal value on the concerns of each human being. This woman faced the very real experience of being dismissed because of her economic class, gender, and race. As a poor woman of color she faced triple jeopardy. The social hierarchies of society can mar and block the reflection of the divine in our humanity. Gender, sexual orientation, physical or mental abilities, physical appearance, racial designation, class status, and many other things affect how society determines our value—and influence our perception of an individual's worth. Can we accept others as human without embracing our own basic humanness? Does self-acceptance precede accepting others?

During that year in New York, I experienced a tension between the affirmation of my personhood and feelings of rejection and isolation due to my religious identity. I sensed the simultaneous duality of being fully embraced and partially embraced. I was fortunate to have the Harlem experience to counter the experience of exclusion. We all need the experience of a homecoming with our humanity. We all do count. We arrive on this earth as human beings. Then society limits our grandeur as individuals created in the very image of God by reducing us, as in my case, to white, male, middle-class, and Protestant. A whisper in the distant realms of our minds reminds us that we are more than this. Sometimes we are not even aware of what motivates us to search for that something. We hunger for a reunion with our primal sense of self as a child of God. A transformation occurs in the depths of our soul when we are treated as human beings, children of God, and we then treat our fellow human beings in like manner. As the arms of God, we need to embrace each other as images of the divine. We need to see ourselves and others through the eyes of God. We can become a new creation, experience a reunion with our divine image—a homecoming with our humanity.

✳✳✳

I left New York City after serving for a year at the Congregational Church of God and at Covenant House. During the subsequent years, I have visited New York numerous times, staying at the Covenant House Faith Community or with friends who were former community members. Covenant House Faith Community members embraced me fully as their Christian brother even when we differed on theology. On Sundays I would attend the morning worship service at the Congregational Church of God.

Pastor Levorn Aaron died in 2000. Covenant House founder Father Bruce Ritter died a year earlier in 1999. Their deaths affected me very differently. I learned of Ritter's death some time after the fact. Bruce Ritter had left Covenant House in disgrace in 1990. Charges of sexual misconduct with youth housed at the agency and questions of financial impropriety with donated funds led to his resignation. While Ritter never acknowledged the legitimacy of the charges—in fact he denied them—there was evidence against him. After leaving Covenant House, Ritter disappeared to a quiet life in rural upstate New York. As the founder of Covenant House, he had been exalted as a saint by thousands, yet he died in obscurity.

I never was close to Bruce Ritter. I had admired him as a man who exemplified compassion for at-risk young people. We shared some good conversations around the dinner table. When my parents visited Covenant House for a few days, Ritter even complimented my mother on the popcorn treat she had prepared to share with community members. (I had to wake my parents at night so Ritter could express his appreciation.) A year after leaving Covenant House, I considered moving back to New York and enrolling in seminary. So I met with Fr. Ritter in his office to discuss a possible return to Covenant House as a Protestant chaplain to the youth at the Under 21 shelter.

When Bruce Ritter was charged with sexually abusing young men at the shelter—and then resigned—I felt shock, betrayal, and embarrassment. I could hardly fathom what he allegedly had done. There were times when I had questioned his viewpoints, judgment, management style, and promotional tactics. He seemed too cozy with wealthy donors whose

lifestyles, political views, and corporate ethics were antitheti-
cal to the commitment to social justice that was at the core
of the identity of Covenant House Faith Community. He ran
Covenant House as a benevolent dictator, which differed from
the egalitarianism of the Covenant House Faith Community.
I had even discovered an old folder that contained an early
draft of Covenant House's history that told of another priest
who worked with Ritter to found the organization. This had
been erased from the history and public relations material
that promoted the myth of Ritter as the solo founder. But
even with these concerns and disagreements, I never would
have thought that Father Bruce Ritter was capable of sexually molesting children—even while he claimed to be rescuing
these same children from the exploitation of the sex industry.

A former coworker described for me the day Bruce Ritter left Covenant House. He said Ritter left quietly in jeans
and a hooded sweatshirt, walking through the Port Authority
bus station unrecognized. Then he added, "Father Ritter had
once been considered the Mother Teresa of America. Now
if anyone would have recognized him they would have spit
on him." I felt as though a part of my life history had been
rewritten, and I had no control over the process. In many
ways Bruce Ritter's death occurred in my life in 1990.

How different it was in December 2000 when I returned to
New York City to participate in the funeral of Levorn Aaron.
Pastor Aaron was eighty years old when he died. I had visited
Aaron and the Congregational Church of God on numerous
occasions since leaving New York in 1982. I had an open invitation to preach whenever I was in the area. I accepted that
invitation many times. I brought my new wife to meet my New
York church family. I sought Dr. Aaron's advice when making decisions. The church was full the day of the funeral, and
many pastors were in attendance. I read a Scripture passage
early in the service and then was invited to offer some brief

reflections at another point in the service when ministers representing different ministerial associations gave remarks. I was introduced as a son of the Congregational Church of God.

The most moving part of the service for me was at the end. The casket, which had been closed during the service, was opened again for everyone to have a final viewing of the body. The ushers directed people, row by row, to walk by and say a final goodbye to Levorn Aaron. Many greeted members of the family who were sitting in the front row before they approached the casket. Finally the ministers were called to walk by the casket. I stopped to speak to Mrs. Aaron and their five daughters (one son died previously and the other son was very ill at home). I did not recall ever having met any of Reverend Aaron's daughters. Yet each of them hugged me and greeted me as "Curt" (which was what Pastor Aaron called me). Each of them said, in almost the same words, "Curt, our Dad loved you so much!" Then they would mention how much he talked about me and how they had seen all of our family photos sent to the Aarons each Christmas. I maintained my composure throughout the service—until I spoke with the family. Homecoming! I rediscovered my humanity in Harlem because a congregation and a pastor embraced me fully as their son and brother and minister.

CHAPTER TWO

Linked to a Lineage of Mentors

My father's family was nurtured in a small Dutch community in rural Kansas. A sign that reads "Prairie View—A Touch of Dutch" greets visitors to this Dutch enclave. My great grandparents, Pieter and Della DeJong, moved to Prairie View in 1895 to work as homesteaders and farmers. Pieter DeJong had arrived in the United States from the Netherlands in 1866 at the age of fourteen. Many Reformed Traditionalists were immigrating to the United States in order to escape the persecution of a state-controlled church. After the death of his first wife, Pieter married my great-grandmother and, with the five children from his first marriage, moved to Prairie View. Ten more children were born to Pieter and Della after they moved to Kansas. My grandfather, Herbert, was among the DeJong children who stayed in the area. He and Letitia (Roberts) raised six children. After Herbert's death in his early fifties, my grandmother and her children moved away from the home place in Kansas.

My life's journey finds roots in a family history of struggle and hard times. The voyage across the Atlantic from the Netherlands to the United States was a tragic one for the DeJongs. Three of Pieter's siblings died of cholera. Their suffering did not end after arriving on the North American shore. Pieter's first wife Anna died at a young age. After he married Della Vanderbeek, tragedy visited them three times in less than ten years: their two-year-old daughter Gracie drowned; a twenty-one-year-old son from the first marriage named Peter died of appendicitis; and their six-year-old son David also died of drowning. My grandmother Letitia was also a great example of perseverance. Left with six children to bring up and support after my grandfather's death, she worked many jobs so that each of her children could attend college.

My ecumenical spirit is nurtured by my family history. One could assume that Dutch immigrants would remain a part of the Reformed Church. Freedom of religion was why many had left the Netherlands. Interestingly, many members of my family joined other denominations. My grandparents joined a Church of God congregation after the birth of their first daughter. Others in the extended family joined Methodist, Baptist, Assemblies of God, and other churches.

I would have thought that Dutch culture would continue to be a major influence in the lives of the DeJong clan. The first generation in the United States did live in Dutch communities, but the appeal of assimilation was strong. The children of Pieter DeJong all changed their surname to DeYoung—the anglicized form. A brother-in-law of Pieter DeJong was even named Benjamin Franklin Vanderbeek. As the years passed, more of the children left the Prairie View community and their Dutch ethnic culture. When the DeJong family arrived in the United States, their values were rooted in Dutch identity and culture. This decreased with each generation until very little of the Dutch culture and identity remains a part of my life in the form of cultural practices and celebrations.

This transformation may have occurred because of leaving the Dutch Reformed Church, since religious tradition often preserves culture. Within my family, church heritage is stronger than Dutch lineage. When my grandmother left the Dutch enclave of Prairie View, Kansas, she moved to Anderson, Indiana, the headquarters of the Church of God. She worked at a

Church of God college while all six of her children attended the school. Many of her grandchildren have also attended Anderson University, beginning with the oldest, myself, to the youngest, my cousin Keena. Our family identity is more deeply rooted in Church of God tradition than Dutch heritage.

The changes in identity have also been evident in marriages. My grandfather, Herbert, married Letitia Roberts who was Irish and English. All of their children married individuals who were not Dutch. My father, Arnold, married Marylin Curtiss, who is predominately English. I married Karen McBee, who is an African American with some Native American ancestry. My great-grandfather Pieter DeJong probably could not have imagined that among his great-great grandchildren would be Rachel DeYoung and Jonathan DeYoung—two individuals who wear a name that recalls his Dutch culture and Reformed religious tradition. Yet their heritage also includes Native American and African American ancestors (society might define them as black DeYoungs). Their religious tradition is informed by a father who is ordained in the Church of God, attendance at a local congregation that is United Methodist, and enrollment in schools that are Quaker and Roman Catholic.

Since arriving in the United States, our branch of the DeJong family has moved away from a mono-ethnic understanding of itself and embraced a multiethnic family paradigm through marriage to persons of other European ethnic groups. Perhaps my marriage and children will move us toward a multicultural, even multiracial, family identity. Maybe this process has predisposed me to a desire for reconciliation and a need to rediscover my full humanity.

I could also tell stories of suffering, perseverance, culture, and faith from my mother's side of the family. My first name is my mother's maiden name—Curtiss. So I have a family-tree name. Both sides of my family have provided me with building blocks for a foundation that has produced my cur-

rent worldview. Yet my family of origin did not have all of the
resources I needed. No matter how wonderful our heritage
may be, our family of origin can also limit and confine our
understanding of humanity.

My notion of family has expanded over time and this process created new possibilities. This has been most apparent
through contact with mentors. My mentors have been like
parental figures in my life. In addition to my parents, in-laws,
aunts, uncles, and grandparents, I have been blessed with
additional family members through mentorship. My relationship with Reverend Levorn Aaron from the Congregational
Church of God in Harlem lasted until his death in 2000. His
investment in my life was one of many gifts I received from
mentors. Mentors have affected my life and work profoundly.
They offered living examples of how to thrive in the settings I
had come to know through experience. In addition to Levorn
Aaron, four other individuals in particular have been key role
models for me at significant points in my life: Calvin Morris, Cain Hope Felder, Samuel Hines, and James Earl Massey.
Interestingly, like Aaron, all are African American males.

Calvin Morris was my professor when I was a seminary student at Howard University School of Divinity. He is a prod-
uct of the civil rights movement. Working with both Martin
Luther King Jr. and Jesse Jackson Sr., he has been at the forefront of a social justice critique of society. Morris brings a
razor sharp ability to cut to the real issues when dealing with
individuals who aspire to leadership. He cared deeply about
his students at Howard University. This concern often trans-
lated into a confrontational style that pressed all of a student's
emotional buttons in a very forceful manner. Morris often
remarked, in essence, "If you cannot take a little pressure at
the seminary, you will never survive in a local congregation."

In my case, Calvin Morris was concerned that, because I
was the son of a pastor, I might be a "daddy's boy." He also

had experienced some legalism in his encounters with congregations in the church communion in which I was raised. He wanted to make sure that I did not have a fundamentalist streak in my theology. Dr. Morris was aware that I planned to work for racial justice, and he wanted to be sure that I was "real" and not just a white-bleeding-heart-do-gooder. He tested me to discover if I could deal with a strong and sometimes angry black male. Morris knew I needed to address some deep issues before I could move forward in the process of working for racial justice and growing in my understanding of leadership.

Calvin Morris performed surgery on my psyche, and he touched a nerve. I found myself growing angry at his constant confrontation. Not only was I upset by his behavior, my annoyance moved to an emotion I had not experienced before—*hatred*. Even now I struggle to write the word "hatred," to admit to that emotion. I soon realized that my disposition affected my seminary coursework and upset my emotional equilibrium. I needed to repent of my hate. And I needed to confess directly to Dr. Morris.

I arranged to meet with him at his office. I confessed my feelings and humbled myself before my professor. After baring my soul, Morris replied that he had been waiting for me to come to him. I perceived his response as arrogant and became even angrier. It was not long before I realized that my desire for forgiveness was not unconditional. Morris was pushing me because he knew I needed to mature. Over time I began to understand that he actually had my best interest in mind. What I experienced as confrontation was really an act of love. I remain grateful to this day that Calvin Morris cared enough about me to invest in my growth as a person and future leader.

Calvin Morris challenged me to critique my presuppositions and unexamined attitudes. Was I willing to make personal changes to emerge as a healthier person ready for lead-

ership? I learned from Morris that leaders who do not exam-
ine themselves and the society in which they live are enslaved
by the status quo. Dr. Morris guided me toward the path of
engaging in life, and the work of reconciliation, as a process.
This process had to begin with me. The dedication in my second book, *Reconciliation: Our Greatest Challenge, Our Only Hope*
reads, "In gratitude to Calvin S. Morris, my friend and mentor, for helping me understand reconciliation as a process."[1]

I also met Cain Hope Felder at Howard University. He
was my New Testament professor at the School of Divinity.
Our life histories were dramatically different. A single mother
raised Cain Hope Felder in Boston, Massachusetts. She named
him Cain to describe the tragic circumstances surrounding
his birth. While Mrs. Felder's husband was hospitalized for an
extended time, his brother raped her, resulting in the birth of
Cain. She named her son Cain because she felt like a brother
had murdered his brother. Although Mrs. Felder had a limited
formal education, her theological instincts were sharp. When
Cain became a teenager, his mother told him the story of his
birth. She said that if he allowed his second name "Hope" to
inform his first name "Cain," God would bless his future.

When I encountered Cain Hope Felder, he was intent on
changing the theological academy. His book *Troubling Biblical
Waters: Race, Class, and Family*, was aimed at scholars trapped in
Eurocentric understandings of the biblical tradition.[2] Felder
discovered a great interest in his work at the grassroots level (he
later edited the *Original African Heritage Bible* to reach this audience).[3] Whether directed toward the academic or the grassroots community, Felder always educates for social change.
He knows that transformation depends on education—teaching new knowledge and reclaiming lost truths. Cain Felder is
passionate about a reconciliation that emerges from the context of social justice praxis. He influenced my commitment
to the academy as a place for preparing social change-mak-

ers. Much of my writing owes its biblical interpretation and truth telling passion to Dr. Felder's important contributions to scholarship and to my life. Cain Hope Felder has inspired me not to fear the path of radical knowledge and revolutionary ideas, as well as to hold on to hope when engaging in prophetic discourse.

Samuel Hines was the mentor who guided me to the path where my ministry was headed: reconciliation. Dr. Hines often said, "God has a one-item agenda: reconciliation."[4] He believed that we live as peacemakers in the midst of the tensions in society created by race, class, gender, and culture. Born and raised in Jamaica, he left his pastoral ministry on the island nation to accept a call to be the senior pastor of Third Street Church of God in Washington, DC. Hines observed a troubling gap between the powerless and the powerful. These two worlds were clearly evident in the twelve blocks separating the neighborhood of Third Street Church of God and the United States Capitol building. Samuel Hines experimented with new processes for social change. He believed that changed individuals led to changed communities and societies. One of his unique efforts at reconciliation was an urban prayer breakfast program for poor and homeless people that brought together the nation's power brokers and the homeless of Washington, DC.

Of particular note was the behind-the-scenes leadership of Hines to help dismantle apartheid in South Africa. He visited numerous times and worked in partnership with several of the leaders of the struggle. His expository preaching on reconciliation changed the lives of many. I have heard testimony to this fact from leaders I have met in South Africa. Rev. Hines also challenged those in his congregation. As a seminary intern at Third Street Church of God, I listened as members described the effect of his reconciliation preaching. One member of the congregation informed me that that she had hated white people until she faced the convincing and compelling preaching of Dr. Samuel Hines.

For three years I served side by side with Hines at the urban prayer breakfast and in the life of the congregation. I learned from an artisan of reconciliation the attitudes and attributes needed for a ministry of reweaving the fabric of broken relationships. Pastor Hines (as many of us called him) mentored me at Third Street Church of God, officiated at my wedding to Karen, laid hands on me in ordination, and counseled me regarding major decisions in my life. I still deeply miss him since his sudden and unexpected death on January 6, 1995.

Also laying hands on me in ordination was James Earl Massey. He is the mentor I have known the longest. I first met Dr. Massey in the fall of 1976 when I was a student at Anderson College in Indiana. He was our campus pastor and professor of biblical studies, while simultaneously serving as the senior pastor of the Metropolitan Church of God in Detroit. I enrolled in one of his courses, and thus our relationship began. Dr. Massey was in his mid forties, and I was eighteen years old. James Earl Massey, like Aaron and Hines, was a "father in the ministry" (a term of affection used for a man who mentors someone in church ministry in a way that merges the roles of father and mentor—a woman mentor would be a "mother in the ministry"). Massey preached at my ordination service in 1985. His preaching and pastoral wisdom have enriched me through the years. James Massey is at home in his identity as a human created in the image of God—he delights in being a child of God. At key moments he has provided me with wisdom both in words and in example. I am heavily indebted to him in ways that words fall short of communicating. The person I am today is a result of being one of the many women and men mentored by James Earl Massey.

In the more than thirty years I have known him and observed his lifestyle, James Earl Massey has excelled at the ethical practice of leadership as a preacher, pastor, professor, dean, civil rights leader, and scholar. Dr. Massey's personal standard of morality is high. He understands well the need for boundaries in relationships. He also believes that personal morality cannot be separated from a commitment to an ethical stance regarding society. I am fortunate to have encountered him at a formative point in my journey. Like James Earl Massey, I have attempted to ground my leadership practice in a faith-inspired ethical commitment that integrates both the personal and social dimensions. James Earl Massey has guided me along the path of integrity, where we embrace others and ourselves as bearers of God's image.

❋❋❋

If the adventure of life leads us into new experiences and different settings, our family of origin likely will not contain all of the cultural, psychological, or even spiritual resources we require. Sometimes our familial bonds can decrease rather than enlarge our life agenda. Certainly the geographic locale of our upbringing, the ethnic cultural heritage that claims us, or the advantage or lack of it that results from our race, gender, and socioeconomic class define the parameters of our possibilities. Our places of belonging must grow in number in order for our opportunities to expand.

In my experience mentors have been critical on the journey. In some cases friends have been the link to new worlds. If we choose to embrace the big world we live in, we must learn from and love folks from places and experiences that enrich us. It is so valuable to be mentored by persons of different races and cultures. What a gift it is for men to be guided by women. When we link to folks from other traditions, they deposit treasures into our lives.

We can be mentored also by the dead, by those who have gone before us. For many years I found the lives and writings of

Dietrich Bonhoeffer, Malcolm X, and Martin Luther King Jr.
very instructive. Each lived for thirty-nine years. As I approached
my fortieth birthday, I needed to find some additional examples.
This kind of disciplined study of the lives of others can take us
into new worlds and even to situations similar to what we face.
Often presidents of the United States read the biographies of
their predecessors or those of other world leaders to gain insight.
Some people find biblical characters helpful guides. Muslims
study the life of Muhammad for clues on how to live.

I contend that if we are to embrace our full humanity, we
must expand our definition of family and community—of
those we invite to speak into our journey. Howard Thurman
wrote, "The willingness to be to another human being what is
needed at the time the need is most urgent and most acutely
felt—this is to participate in a precise act of redemption. This
is to stand for one intimate moment in loco dei in the life of
another— that is, to make available to another what has already
been given us."[5] Each of the mentors I have noted stood in my
life and passed on to me what had been given to them. It was
an act of amazing generosity on their part for which I am eter-
nally grateful. Can I stand in the life of others?

I have also been a mentor for the past several years. This is a
high honor and humbling call. It is a frightening prospect to be
trusted by another in this manner. Among those who have sought
my guiding insights on a regular basis are women and men, folks
from differing races, even persons from other countries. At fifty
years of age, I stand at a unique place where I am called upon to
be a mentor while still an active recipient of mentoring.

✳✳✳

My family of origin provided me with a wonderful history
and a strong foundation of love. Mentors have contributed an
important added dimension to my heritage. Not only have my
mentors bestowed upon me additional parental figures or sig-

nificant role models; they have connected me to an expanded and very rich legacy. For example, through my relationship with James Earl Massey, I am linked to Howard Thurman, who was a primary mentor to Massey. Thurman was an African American mystic-activist and theologian who influenced Martin Luther King Jr. and many of the key leaders of the civil rights movement. Howard Thurman was a preacher, prophet, and practitioner of reconciliation. He passionately searched for the common ground of human community and the experience of knowing oneself to be fully human as God intended—something his grandmother, a woman freed from slavery, pined for. Reconciliation was integrated into all of his work as a theologian, pastor, and professor.

Mary McLeod Bethune was a mentor to Thurman during his youth. He attended her school in Daytona, Florida. Bethune was born to parents who had been enslaved in the Southern United States. She believed that education enabled one to embrace her or his own sense of worth, respond to racism, and succeed in a country beset with racial injustice. Mary McLeod Bethune's faith was the bedrock of her efforts.

Sojourner Truth's life inspired Bethune to develop leaders. Sojourner Truth was born into slavery and escaped as an adult. As the result of a vision, she took the name Sojourner Truth to replace her slave name. In the vision God told her that she would sojourn in the land proclaiming God's truth. Sojourner Truth spent her life serving God as a trumpet of truth against racism and sexism. I am not aware of Sojourner Truth mentioning human mentors. That does not mean that she was without a mentor. According to Sojourner Truth, she was mentored directly by Jesus Christ. This reminds us that all of the human help we gain from mentors does not replace a direct relationship with God.[6]

Through my relationship with James Earl Massey, I have been enriched by aspects of the wisdom handed down from

Sojourner Truth to Mary McLeod Bethune, from Bethune to Howard Thurman, and from Thurman to James Earl Massey. This is an amazing and humbling gift from God. The Hebrew Psalmist wrote, "You have given me the heritage of those who fear your name" (61:5). This lineage of mentors is an unfathomable gift with a value beyond my ability to comprehend. I thank God for such a blessing. Most of us need such a heritage if we are going to reach our full potential as human beings created in the image of God.

The richness of a mentoring lineage struck me powerfully on two separate occasions. I was honored for ten years of executive leadership with the Twin Cities Urban Reconciliation Network (TURN) in 2001. Dr. James Earl Massey was the preacher for the celebration worship event. Before preaching a magnificent sermon on reconciliation, he made some personal remarks. He said, "In the fifty years of my married life to Gwendolyn Inez, we lost five children. The first two were a set of twins. Therefore, we have gone into the years without the blessing of children and are now at that far end of life where we understand the joy of togetherness. But if I had had a son, and if it had been my privilege to custom-make that son, he would have been a young man like Curtiss Paul DeYoung. I say no more. No more needs to be said on that. I have never said that about anyone else."[7] I was completely overwhelmed and emotionally moved by Dr. Massey's kind and generous comments.

In early 2002, I read a copy of James Massey's newly released autobiography, *Aspects of my Pilgrimage*. I came to a section where he described an event that celebrated his twenty-fifth anniversary of ordination to the Christian ministry. Howard Thurman was unable to attend, so he sent a letter to be read at the event. At the end of the letter, Thurman made these remarks regarding Massey, "On this occasion, therefore, I salute you as a blood brother of the mind *and* spirit. If it had been my portion to have had a son and, as a part of the discreetness of life I had been privileged to custom-make him, he would be a young man like you. I say no more; no more is necessary to say."[8]

CHAPTER THREE

A "White" Malcolm X

In 1983 I enrolled as a student at the Howard University School of Divinity in Washington, DC, a premiere historically African American institution of higher learning. I was one of only a few full-time, traditional students who were white and the only white person in most of my classes. While I was initially uncomfortable in my newfound minority status, this experience proved to be a priceless gift for my learning process. After a few class sessions, it was as though my presence was no longer noticed, and I began to hear very blunt and honest conversations concerning racism and life in the African American community. This is an unusual experience for a white person. Often when whites are present, persons of color change or edit their conversations—especially when it deals with matters of racism. This also occurs in white circles when a person of color is present. Therefore, authentic dialogue on racism rarely occurs. I gained many of my insights regarding racism in society during my time at Howard University, through formal class settings and informal conversations. I was also schooled in the perspectives of the African American church, black liberation theology, Afrocentric biblical interpretation, and the prophetic black preaching tradition. I gained candid insights on how racism invades every part of the life of African Americans.

I also discovered during my tenure at Howard University that the longer I was around the hallways and classrooms of the seminary the more I simply became a part of the community. This was evident in many ways, particularly through friendships forged with students and faculty. A course taught by Dr. Calvin Morris provides an example of this process of being acculturated into the community. Professor Morris was a veteran of the civil rights movement, having served under both Martin Luther King Jr. with the Southern Christian Leadership Conference (SCLC) and Jesse Jackson Sr. with Operation PUSH. Later he was the executive director at the Martin Luther King Jr. Center for Social Change in Atlanta, Georgia, and on staff at Ebenezer Baptist Church, whose senior pastor was Daddy King (the father of M. L. King Jr.). Also enrolled in Morris's course was Bernard Lee, another veteran of the civil rights movement. Rev. Lee was one of Martin Luther King Jr.'s closest friends and his constant traveling companion in King's final years. Lee had promised Dr. King that one day he would attend seminary. Finally in the mid 1980s, he was fulfilling that promise when I arrived as a student.

On breaks during class sessions it was a delight to hear Calvin Morris and Bernard Lee swap stories about movement days. Dr. Morris and Rev. Lee had a playful and affectionate side to their banter. Using language common to their era, they would affectionately refer to each other as "Negro" in place of their names (for example, "This Negro said. . ."). As one enthralled by the study of the civil rights movement, I often would be at the edge of their conversations, hanging on every word. Soon I was included in the banter as well. First they referred to me as "this white Negro." It was not long until I was referred to as "Negro" in the same way they referred to each other. Obviously, I was affirmed and flattered at how they included me fully in their circle.

Black colleagues and friends through the years have expressed similar sentiments. I have been introduced in African American settings as white on the outside but black on the inside. When I left an organization that was trying to increase the percentage of persons of color employed, I remarked that my leaving would help the organization meet this goal. An African American coworker informed me that I did not count as white. This even occurs outside of the United States. I was called a white soul brother by a Jamaican colleague and a black South African wrote to me, "I say to you may the good God bless you, stay as a black man in a white skin."

Of course this is all very affirming. It is a tribute to the fact that I have been immersed in the African American community for a significant portion of my life. I have gone to great lengths in listening to and learning from persons of many races and cultures. Not only did this education occur in Harlem and at Howard University but also at Wounded Knee on the Pine Ridge Indian Reservation, in the Hmong communities of St. Paul and Minneapolis, and in various Latina/o settings. I have invited women to speak truth into my life. African Americans have mentored me. I have submitted to the authority of persons of color and women at work, church, and in life. I have read widely and discussed endlessly the perspectives informed by worldviews shaped in cultures and settings unlike my own.

In fact, due to my Howard University training and subsequent research, I may hold a more radical black liberationist perspective than many African Americans. Afrocentric biblical scholar Cain Hope Felder wrote in the foreword of my first book, "Here are the fruits and scholarship of a European-American minister and social activist who has uniquely chosen to sit where many so-called minorities have had to sit. He thereby writes as one who knows what it is to be an alien in your native land and to some extent marginalized because of choosing to break from the pack and to look at the social chaos and injustice of those below who hurt."[1]

Yet I am still a white male! I may have acquired an intellectual stance usually reserved for persons of color and even acculturated some patterns from other cultures (especially in my preaching), but I will never experience life as a person of color. As a white male in the United States, I benefit from a history and present reality that has given me significant advantages and privileges. I am also protected from the many daily indignities and reduction of life choices experienced by others because of racism, sexism, and injustice.

Yes, I had previously experienced something similar to second-class citizenship as a Protestant in a Roman Catholic community. And yes, I felt pain and carried scars because of that encounter. But I always had options. I was free to leave at any time. I could have converted to Catholicism to secure participation at the communion table in the Covenant House Faith Community. I found that upon my return to mainstream society, my status as a Protestant actually serves as advantage in the United States. Likewise, I was a minority while at Howard University. I experienced a certain amount of discomfort initially, and for a time I felt like an outsider. But I departed from minority status every time I walked out of the confines of the university. I was free at any time to leave my "minority" position. Clearly however, switching skin color to secure some of the advantages I have due to my white skin was never an option for my fellow students, professors, or even the dean at Howard University School of Divinity.

Perhaps as you read about my experience at the church in Harlem, you wondered why I needed to experience what it meant to be human. Don't white, middle-class males already enjoy that privilege? One easily could make the case that in the United States of America white, middle-class males are the norm, the default mode, and society's definition of what it means to be human. But I have discovered that, while white males historically created a system that they continue to dominate and benefit from, we are also hurt by it. The following episode illustrates this.

To my surprise, while visiting New York City a few years ago, I discovered that I had been affected by racism. A coworker asked me to purchase a hat for him called a kufi. He said that such a hat could be found at a marketplace near the Apollo Theater in the heart of Harlem. I had been in Harlem on a regular basis during my tenure at the Congregational Church of God. While I had never been to this particular section of Harlem before, I had always been at ease as a white person in this African American cultural Mecca. As I stepped out of the entrance to the subway station on a sunny summer day, I was excited to be back in Harlem. The marketplace was abuzz with vendors selling shirts that displayed Malcolm X's face and items that exhibited the colors of Africa.

As soon as I walked out onto the streets of Harlem, I was gripped by an intense and emotionally raw fear. I quickly searched for the hat I came to buy. I did not see a pretty sun-lit day in New York. I saw rage on the face of Malcolm X peering at me from a T-shirt and crying out, "By any means necessary." I felt intimidated as the only white person in a sea of hundreds of black people. While I had experienced discomfort and anxiety during my first few days at Howard University, I had never felt fearful.

All of the negative social images I had acquired about African Americans were projected on the movie screen of my mind. I frantically attempted to regain control of my thoughts and emotions. I reminded myself that I had no reason to fear. I panicked even though I had not been threatened. The marketplace was in a safe section of Harlem. People were shopping or attending to their daily activities. I analyzed my thoughts and emotions as I anxiously walked the streets of Harlem. My imagination had been seized by deeply ingrained stereotypes I somehow had absorbed.

I said to myself that the people I saw in Harlem that day were not plotting revenge against me because of my white

skin. A white man walking the streets of Harlem did not natu-
rally lead to an act of wanton violence or verbal harassment.
Yet I could not free myself from these debilitating feelings of
fear. Unable to restore my emotional equilibrium, or find the
hat, I sought out a police officer for information. Although the
police officer was an African American, his "blue" uniform
counteracted his "black" skin and made him safe in the midst
of my emotional turmoil. I inquired if he knew where I might
find a kufi. He was not aware where I might find such an item.
So I gave up on securing the hat, left Harlem, and my emotional disruption subsided.

As I rode the subway back to the lower part of Manhattan
and away from Harlem, I was troubled that my life experience
and belief in reconciliation did not prevent my intense response.
I felt embarrassed by my reaction that day. How could I experience such feelings when I had been married to an African
American woman for several years and we had children who
were defined by some as black? I certainly did not embrace
any of the stereotypes that had dominated my thoughts on this
visit to Harlem. Finally, I realized that I needed healing from
inherited beliefs and irrational fears that resulted from being
raised in white society. Even as a white person in the United
States, I had been wounded by racism, albeit unknowingly. I
am certain that I am not alone in this experience. Many whites
are not aware of the invisible scars they carry on their souls
due to racism and unearned privilege.[2]

In addition to the fears and wounds that accompany
privilege, whites, like persons of color, are locked into "their
place." I noted earlier that many people have affirmed my
efforts to let go of white privilege and live in solidarity with
persons of color. But I have learned that I cannot just throw
away my whiteness. Some persons of color make assumptions
about me simply because I am white: I am automatically a
racist; I cannot possibly understand their struggles because I

was raised white; I have power in society because I am white. It would seem that as a white male I too could be judged by the color of my skin. I once mentioned this to a close friend of color and was offered no sympathy. I was informed that people of color go through this every day. Of course I already knew that. I guess I was hoping for some empathy or compassion from someone who knows how it feels. Instead, I felt further demeaned.

I do not recount the "challenges" of being white to gain sympathy. But I have discovered the reality that white males striving for racial reconciliation and social justice face unique challenges. Certainly, people of color working for racial reconciliation face significantly more severe challenges due to historic and present racism. Yet as a white male I have to remain committed to persevere and tough it out. I have to close my ears to the beckoning and tempting cries of white privilege to return to an "easier" life of racial advantage. I also have to "prove" myself over and over again. Some persons of color may never fully trust me because I am white. It is useless to cry over these issues. The legacy of racism demands more of me. I am paying for the sins of my white forefathers. Facing the challenges and not giving up are part of the process of real reconciliation for white persons.

I stated at the outset of this chapter that I studied at the Howard University School of Divinity in Washington, DC. The real reason I enrolled was not because I was eager to study at Howard University. Actually, I was not even aware that Howard University had a school of divinity. This is not knowledge that most whites gain in their process of searching for a seminary. The racial segregation in our society even affects the information we receive about graduate education. This lack of knowledge proves itself occasionally when I say I graduated from Howard University. Some white person will think I must have said Harvard University, and they are quite

impressed. When I correct them they seem surprised or perhaps even disappointed.

Previously, I had been accepted into the Masters of Divinity program at Union Theological Seminary and the Masters
of Social Work program at Columbia University in New York
City. I had planned to return to New York, attend these fine
institutions, and continue my ministry apprenticeship with
Rev. Levorn Aaron and the Congregational Church of God
in Harlem. Before the planned move back to New York City
was to occur, I landed a three-month internship at the Third
Street Church of God in Washington, DC, where Samuel
Hines was the senior pastor. I felt fortunate to be able to add
this experience to my previous urban endeavors before returning to New York.

On my first Sunday at this congregation comprised of
African Americans and persons from the Caribbean, I met
a beautiful young woman named Karen McBee. Within a
few weeks we were dating. I quickly had a decision to make.
Should I maintain my plans to move to New York City and
try a commuter relationship? Two ministers on staff at Third
Street Church of God recommended that I consider Howard
University School of Divinity. So I spoke to the dean of the
school of divinity, Dr. Lawrence Jones. I discovered in our conversation that he had previously served at Union Theological
Seminary in New York. Dean Jones assured me that Howard
University would welcome my enrollment. In a matter of two
weeks, I was accepted into Howard University and decided
to remain in Washington, DC. The church gladly extended
my internship. All of this happened because I had become
imprisoned by my affections for this twenty-three-year-old
woman. Sometimes God uses matters of the heart to gain our
attention and order the steps of our lives.

This decision was not only significant because it caused
me to alter my plans but because I had just crossed a line.

Racism even affects the world of intimate relationships: marriage, parenting, and friendships. Interracial relationships did
not just happen in the early 1980s. You entered them aware
of the realities of a racially divided society. The first time we
were alone together was at dinner at a Houlihans restaurant
in Washington, DC, a few weeks after we first met. We had
been together in group settings in the intervening days. We
had no idea how the other person viewed dating and marriage outside of one's racial group. In order to proceed in the
relationship, we needed to have a discussion. I do not remember who brought it up that night at the restaurant, but we both
declared our openness to and interest in moving forward. So
dinner that night *became* our first date.

Our relationship jelled quickly. We both had significant
experience in relating outside our racial and cultural group.
Pastor Samuel Hines informed us in the premarital counseling sessions that he was surprised and delighted by the degree
of our compatibility. At times we would forget the racial difference. On one occasion when Karen and I attended a gathering, she noted that there were no whites in attendance. She
had forgotten that I was white.

Our wedding was a biracial event. We both included African
Americans and whites in our choice of who would be members of the wedding party. When the wedding party exited following the ceremony—with the exception of the best man and
maid of honor, and our parents—each couple was interracial
(this was not planned and went unnoticed until we watched
the wedding video). To add to this poignant moment, as our
pastor Samuel Hines brought up the rear of the recessional
my grandmother stepped out and put her arm through his and
recessed out with him as the final interracial couple.

Others have not always embraced our crossing of the racial
line. People have stared at us. Both whites and African Americans have shared their displeasure with our choice to date and

marry. Sometimes comments have been expressed with crass-ness. Once an African American male shouted at us, "What the f--- are you doing with one of the sisters?" Another time while we were strolling through a park hand in hand, a group of white males hollered at us from their car, "Gross, sick, disgusting!"

Still our greatest challenge came from the church. While attending seminary, the white pastor of a multiracial con-gregation asked me to consider serving as their youth pastor. White members who believed that our relationship was a bad example for their youth soon nixed this idea. I often filled the pulpit for another nearby congregation that was without a pastor. The congregation was predominantly white with a sprinkling of persons of color. When my name was suggested as a potential part-time pastor, a white leader in this congre-gation spoke against the idea because, in his words, "He has a personal problem." I soon learned that my "personal prob-lem" was my fiancée, Karen.

Karen and I reacted differently to the situation. I stated that we should just call the church leader a "racist jerk" and move on. Karen informed me that I could get rid of her and no longer have "a problem." But her skin color would always be a problem in the opinion of the church leader. Racism affected both our perception of the situation and how we responded emotionally.[3] The incident also taught me that even as a person in an interracial relationship, *I was still white.* I experienced discrimination because of my choice to be in a relationship with Karen. I could end the relationship and be free of the experience of bigotry, but Karen had no choice regarding how she was viewed in these situations. Later, as I searched for a congregational placement following seminary, I always enclosed a photo of Karen and me in order to avoid a repeat of such unpleasant situations.

I face a perplexing predicament. I experience a significant amount of rage at racism, and I experience white privilege because of racism. I constantly have to address the challenge of how to reconcile advantage and anger inwardly. This dichotomy became even clearer to me as I did research for *United by Faith: The Multiracial Congregation as an Answer to the Problem of Race*, a book I coauthored with Michael Emerson, George Yancey, and Karen Chai Kim.[4] I researched a section on the history of racism in Christian congregations in the United States. The poised and neutral perspective of a researcher was replaced by a simmering rage as I read about the brutality of whites toward Native Americans and African Americans in the name of Christ. I read historical accounts of Native Americans and African Americans singing hymns and offering prayers as they were hung, with ropes around their necks from the gallows or from trees, by whites that professed to be Christians. I read how Native Americans and African Americans were segregated into separate seats, separate church buildings, or even separate "praying towns" by whites that claimed to believe in Jesus Christ.

My anger at the Christian church soon led me to sink into a depressed state. I was embarrassed. I was sick to my stomach. I was outraged. I was close to quitting Christianity. I identified with Malcolm X, who was angry at the white racism of Christians and its effect on African Americans. I was caught in a disturbing and disheartening dilemma. People who looked like me slaughtered Native Americans. People from my Dutch and English ethnic heritage captured, enslaved, beat, raped, and lynched persons of African descent. I cannot seem to distance myself from feelings of anger, nor can I escape from the advantage that whiteness bestows on me. I cannot change history and I cannot change the fact that I am white.

I must admit that I sometimes feel like a *white* Malcolm X. Now I do not mean to offend someone by my use of this phrase, "a white Malcolm X." And please do not misunderstand my intentions. Some may have difficulty accepting this idea because Malcolm X is an icon of the African American community. Therefore, a "white Malcolm X" is a contradiction of terms, even offensive. If you are familiar only with misguided media portrayals of Malcolm X as a purveyor of violence, then you will not comprehend this metaphor. You may be unaware of the religious conversion that Malcolm X experienced at the end of his life, while on a pilgrimage to Mecca, that transformed him from a racial separatist to an agent of human rights. So let me tell you what I mean.

I feel like a white Malcolm X because, like Malcolm, I am enraged by racism.

I feel like a white Malcolm X because, like Malcolm, I am frustrated by how white racial superiority and privilege mocks God.

I feel like a white Malcolm X because, like Malcolm, I am compelled to preach the truth and fight for change.

Yes, I often feel like a white Malcolm X. I sometimes ask if it is my whiteness that keeps me committed to reconciliation. If I were not white would I feel obligated to work for reconciliation and a vision of a multicultural community? If I were not white would I actually forgive? I also wonder if being a white male has made it easier to be a Christian. If I were not a white male would I choose to be a Christian, given the church's history of racism and sexism? These questions are difficult for me to answer. Perhaps my stance would parallel that of the pre-Mecca Malcolm X if I were born black. Maybe I would preach separation if I were oppressed.

I have no choice but to work for reconciliation and social justice if I want to rediscover my own humanity as a white male. In his final year of life, Malcolm X had a homecoming of sorts when he went on a pilgrimage to Mecca. I am on a lifelong pilgrimage to be at home with my humanity and my God. Part of my journey requires traveling through the internal tensions between privilege and pain, reconciliation and rage. I believe this path also requires that I synthesize the

disparate and the disturbing elements that are found in the
title of this chapter, *a white Malcolm X!*

✳✳✳

When one's journey toward greater self-knowledge runs parallel to a growing awareness of injustice in society and a firsthand glimpse of the life narratives of those directly affected
by oppression, a dissonance or disruption is bound to occur.
My life sometimes seems like a song played in a key a bit jar-
ring to my own sense of self and certainly for those listening. I
feel like I live in the place of identity chaos where perspectives
collide and viewpoints crash. My white, middle-class origins
whisper an inviting appeal to return to a life of privilege far
away from cries of pain and suffering. My journeys into suffering and injustice call me to solidarity and outrage. How do
I respond to the juxtaposition of comfort and rage?

As a white male with birthright advantage and privilege, I
face this recurring question: Am I trapped forever in "whiteness" and "maleness"? Is this definition of my identity cast in
concrete? Or can I find my true, God-created humanity and
experience a primal homecoming? Is it possible to embrace a
new "view" of myself as a "multicultural" person—not limited by a history of racism created by the system within which
I live? Perhaps the reality for my life and my generation is
choosing to exist in the tension of intentionally living in the
chasm between privilege and oppression.

On the road to Damascus, the Apostle Paul had a homecoming experience that transformed him from a religious
separatist into an ambassador of reconciliation (Acts 9:1-19;
26:13-16). Several years later he reflected on this dramatic
and unexpected change in his life, "But by the grace of God I
am what I am, and his grace toward me has not been in vain"
(1 Corinthians 15:10). By God's grace I have been called to
the ministry of reconciliation. My responsibilities include the

personal ongoing work of reconciling my rage at racism and
the privilege assigned by my whiteness. I believe that our personal growth requires us to become new people. God's grace
must not be in vain.

✳✳✳

In the spring of 2007, my book *Living Faith: How Faith Inspires
Social Justice* was published.[5] The person and message of
Malcolm X played a prominent role in the book. As Fortress
Press sought people to endorse the book, they had the good
fortune of securing an endorsement from Malaak Shabazz,
the youngest daughter of Malcolm X. This was made possible by Dowoti Désir, the executive director of the newly
opened Malcolm X and Dr. Betty Shabazz Memorial and
Educational Center in Harlem. Malaak was recommended
by Dowoti because she had studied her father's life and was
seeking to follow in his footsteps through her work in human
rights. During the course of related conversations, Ms. Désir
suggested that the Shabazz Center might host the launch of
my new book. This was agreed upon by Fortress Press and the
Shabazz Center.

I arrived in Harlem on the evening of April 13, 2007, for
the book launch. This date was chosen to coincide with the
anniversary of Malcolm X's departure in 1964 on the Hajj—
the Islamic pilgrimage to Mecca. This event transformed
Malcolm's life and it symbolized a central argument in my
book about how religious faith inspired and shaped the lives
of social justice activists. Dowoti Désir organized a panel for
the event that evening that included Imam Aiyub Abdul-Baqi,
Dr. Luis Barrios, and Malaak Shabazz, with Ms. Désir serving
as the moderator and also a panel member. They had all read
my book and responded to it at the evening event.

The Shabazz Center is located at the Audubon Ballroom.
This was the venue for many of Malcolm X's final speeches and

the place of his assassination while giving a speech on February 21, 1965. As I entered the doorway to the Shabazz Center, I felt the historic nature of the place. I noticed the kiosks with video footage of Malcolm's life, and I saw the engaging statue of Malcolm X speaking. I walked up the stairs to the second floor and set foot in the ballroom itself. The Audubon Ballroom has been beautifully renovated into a stunning location. The walls are covered with lovely murals depicting different phases of the life of Malcolm X. Despite the enhancements and changes, this was clearly the same ballroom I had seen so many times in documentaries about Malcolm X.

Dowoti Désir met me as I entered the ballroom and commenced to show me around and describe the various murals. Then she paused for a moment and quietly remarked, "This is where Malcolm died." It was a surreal moment to stand in the place where this prophet of truth, justice, and reconciliation breathed his last breath as bullets took away his life. I felt like I was standing on holy ground.

There was still some time before the event began, so I returned to the kiosks on the first floor to watch some of the video of Malcolm speaking. It was not long until a tall confident woman entered through the front door to the Shabazz Center. Although I had never met her, I knew immediately that this was Malaak Shabazz. She looked like her father and had his regal presence about her. I introduced myself and greeted her. Malaak took my hand and thanked me for my book.

Soon the evening event began, with introductions of the panel. We were seated just a foot or two from the spot where Malcolm X died. This awareness remained at the forefront of my thoughts while I spoke, listened, and responded to questions. In some profound sort of quiet and subtle way, Malcolm X seemed present with us. The final response to my book came from Malaak herself. Her words were very affirming. But what struck me most was what I saw, rather than heard.

I looked at her copy of the book and observed how worn and marked up it was. This is the greatest compliment to an author. She later said to me in a side conversation that I had really understood the essence of her father.

When Malcolm X was shot, Malaak and her twin sister Malikah were in the womb of her pregnant mother. Malaak was the last born of the six daughters of Malcolm and Betty Shabazz. In fact the daughters often refer to each other by number, making Malaak "number six." In a final remark at the event, I spoke directly to Malaak. I noted that she never knew her father in the flesh but had studied him and followed in his footsteps working for human rights and justice. I also never met Malcolm X. I did not know who he was until long after my birth. Yet he has had a profound affect on my journey and worldview. His perspective provided for me a symbolic framework for interpreting my own thinking and feelings about reconciliation and rage using the defining metaphor of a "white Malcolm X." Perhaps on that April night at the Audubon Ballroom, a white Malcolm X encountered the black Malcolm X and set sail on a pilgrimage that brought him closer to a homecoming with his humanity and his God.

Chapter Four

Taco Bell Lutheran

W hen I arrived in 1986 as the senior pastor at First Church of God in Minneapolis, Minnesota, little did I know that my pastoral duties would include serving a second congregation, Taco Bell Lutheran. Paul and Anne Thelander could be found here. Anne was a pianist at First Church of God and her husband Paul, a Lutheran preacher's kid, would attend periodically. On most days Paul and Anne, and whoever else joined them, could be found conversing about religion around a table at the neighborhood Taco Bell restaurant. Therefore, at such occasions the restaurant was christened "Taco Bell Lutheran." Other subjects were discussed, but religion was a central discourse. Most of the people who participated in the discussions found themselves at the margins of society due to homelessness or a diagnosis of mental illness. Paul and Anne met while in residence at a hospital psychiatric ward. Both were highly educated. Paul nearly completed a Ph.D. and held some patents on scientific inventions he had developed. Paul and Anne's religious faith prompted them to believe that God cared about persons who were at the margins and that people of faith would act in the same manner. I regularly joined Paul, Anne, and their "congregation" at Taco Bell Lutheran for food, religious discussions, and a sense of community. Taco Bell Lutheran was a church where people society had cast aside could come and know that their voice and personhood counted.

This vision of ministry was familiar to me. I brought a similar vision to Minneapolis from my work in New York City and Washington, DC. Serving at the Congregational Church of God in Harlem and at Covenant House in Times Square taught me that God's presence was found among those who had been marginalized by society because of race, social class, gender, culture, sexual orientation, disability, and lifestyle choices. Working under the ministry leadership of Samuel Hines in Washington, DC, I learned that poverty locked people into lives of desperation or despondency. I was involved in an active ministry to homeless persons at Third Street Church of God—the congregation where Hines was the pastor—through counseling, job referrals, and feeding individuals breakfast five days a week. My wife, Karen, and I also joined a group of church members who delivered sandwiches at night to people sleeping on the streets of the capital city of the richest and most powerful nation in the world. It was not unusual to see stark and troubling contradictions, such as people facing the *injustice* of poverty and homelessness as they lay on the street outside the building that quite comfortably housed the Department of Justice.

Fresh from seminary and ministry in Washington, DC, I arrived in Minneapolis very idealistic. I came with a vision for leading a congregation that would be a beacon of hope in its community and a force for reconciliation and social justice. I began my ministry a few years before the congregation's fortieth anniversary. In many ways the church had changed little since its inception. First Church of God was founded after World War II by a group of people with roots in Scandinavian and German cultural heritage. Most members in the congregation had a conservative outlook, a result of their experience of the economic depression during the first half of the twentieth century in the United States. From the beginning, First Church of God was a tight-knit community of people brought together by common cultural, economic, political, and theological perspectives.

The original leaders of First Church of God shaped a congregational culture based on their Scandinavian and German roots, the experience of an economic depression in the United States during the 1930s and 1940s, a Protestant work ethic, and an inwardly focused moral code. The ethnic culture of the founding members produced a congregation that avoided conflict and public dialogue on divisive or challenging issues. A Protestant work ethic, combined with their experience of the economic depression of the 1930s, created a survival mentality, a large savings account, and a resistance to change and risk taking. The theology of First Church of God usually was demonstrated through personal (rather than social) morality—no smoking, no swearing, no drinking, and so on.

Several of the founding members still occupied powerful leadership positions in the senior years of their lives. The primary change in the congregation was a slow exodus of the founders' children because of the appeal of the suburbs, internal church conflict, or the moral views held by church leadership. During the years prior to my arrival in 1986, two African American families and two interracial couples had joined the congregation. All were members of the denomination who had moved to the area. Simultaneously, the neighborhood surrounding the church building was entering the early stages of a transition from being an exclusively white to a racially integrated community.

The congregation was in decline because of the loss of members and the absence of pastoral leadership for two years. I was hired to preach good sermons, bring in new members (young people), develop fresh leadership, and transform First Church of God into a congregation that reflected its urban multicultural neighborhood. The congregation expected that I would attract young people, since I was young and fresh from the seminary. My urban ministry training and experience were considered a plus for developing an urban multicultural congregation. My interracial marriage was seen as a symbol of the congregation's future. Eighteen months after my arrival, this small congregation of fifty members had nearly doubled in size. Many of the new members were young people. First Church of God, which was 90% white at the time of my commencement as pastor, had become a congregation where 70% were white, 20% were African American, and 10% were Asian. The vision of the congregation was rapidly becoming a reality.

An alternative adult Sunday School class best exemplified how this vision took on flesh. The class was designed to connect individuals going through "twelve step" drug and alcohol addiction recovery programs with the ministry of the church. The format included dialogue and relationship building as central components. Every week there was a time for people to "check in." Each person would share about her or his experiences of pain and joy from the previous week. The alternative class welcomed everybody who showed up. Even if you did not abide by the congregation's moral code, you were still affirmed as a person moving toward faith in God—like everybody else. To the horror of some of the long-term members, individuals from the alternative class might be observed smoking a cigarette on the front steps of the church after the service. The alternative Sunday School class caused members of First Church of God to understand their community in new ways. This class rapidly expanded beyond its original target group to become a representative microcosm of the congregation's growing edge of future members: working class and poor people, people of color, and individuals with little or no religious background.

The congregation faced the challenge of offering ministry that met the needs of people facing a whole new set of social issues. Some of those attending were struggling with drug and alcohol addiction. I reached out in many ways to individuals who found their way to the church through this alternative class. Oftentimes this occurred in less than glamorous ways, like visiting the detox center, seeking to save marriages where cocaine addiction was destroying trust, and intervening in domestic abuse situations. The ministry initiated by the alternative class was clear evidence that some in the congregation had a very wide view of who belonged at First Church of God. A small revolution was occurring within the congregation. The distance between First Church of God and Taco Bell Lutheran was shrinking.

The entire feel of the congregation's ministry was being transformed. The children's ministry was among the first to experience the change. A woman living on public assistance brought the daughter of a neighboring family to Sunday School. The girl and her family had recently arrived as refugees from Southeast Asia. Soon this young girl's brothers and sisters were also attending, along with several of their friends. Members of the congregation picked up the children in their cars until a van was purchased. After the children began attending, some teenagers and a few adults followed them. Many of the adults struggled with understanding English—and the congregation was not prepared to offer translation into Hmong—so their attendance was sporadic. But First Church of God was their church home. They continued to send their children to church services and identified me as their pastor by seeking out my counsel and inviting me to attend family celebrations. This congregation started by Scandinavians and Germans now had a children's choir that was primarily comprised of the daughters and sons of these Hmong families. Teenagers were baptized and babies were dedicated in Sunday services. One family even named their newborn daughter Ka to honor my wife Karen.

A growing number of African American families also began attending the congregation. New worship styles, such as black gospel music, were introduced to create a more relevant setting for incoming members. Some saw these new worship rituals as competing with the existing and "approved" repertoire of musical selections. As a result of my training at Howard University School of Divinity, my sermons were different in style and sermon content from previous pastors. One African American member of the congregation noted that I preached with a black preacher's cadence but had a white face. He considered this as ideal for an emerging multiracial church. The call and response of traditional African American congregations was introduced at First Church of God. It was not unusual to hear an "Amen" or "Hallelujah" in response to a point made in a sermon. The content of my sermons often focused on issues of social justice and racism. This was quite a departure from the normal fare of sermons that exclusively addressed personal lifestyle concerns. African American preachers were also invited as guest speakers.

One result of the demographic changes occurring in the congregation was that racial tensions simmered just below the surface. First Church of God began celebrating the Sunday of the Martin Luther King Jr. holiday in January with sermons that related to King's life. One white person grumbled, after a few years of this, "Is it *already* time for *another* one of those King days?" Another white parishioner complained on a survey distributed to the congregation that I spent too much time with black people in the church. It was noted by the group analyzing the survey that this was hard for the pastor to avoid since the other people who lived in his home—his wife and children—were black.

My leadership style initially caused some confusion. I had worked in African American congregations where the pastor was given great latitude to move ahead on programming. At First Church of God most of the power for decision-making was in the hands of the lay leadership. In fact, there was a lack of trust in pastors because of a rapid turnover of pastors in the past, with many pastors staying less than three years. (A bishop does not appoint pastors in the Church of God. Rather they are selected by the local congregation and are free to leave when they choose or as the congregation determines.) My fast-paced style of implementation conflicted with the slow deliberate process of the lay leadership.

The diverse growth during the first eighteen months of my leadership at First Church of God included the arrival of many people unlike the founding members—African Americans (middle-class, working-class, and poor), refugees from Southeast Asia, and white working-class and poor people. Some of these new congregants had little or no church background. Initially this change in the make up of the congregation was celebrated as an exciting opportunity to realize God's vision for reconciliation and unity. As the congregation became more racially, culturally, and economically diverse, a few long-term members subtly posed the question: Who were the "real members" of First Church of God? The shifts that occurred during those first eighteen months moved the congregation into an identity crisis.

The existence of many cultures side by side at First Church of God caused a number of fault lines to appear. In the view of some, a hierarchy based on race, culture, economics, and denominational heritage implied one's status or social standing in the congregation. The hierarchy of value was constructed as follows (with 1 as the most valued):

1.   Whites who were denomination members from birth
2.   Whites who joined the denomination
3.   Middle-class whites

4. Middle-class African Americans who were
    members of the denomination
5. Middle-class African Americans
6. Low-income and poor whites
7. Refugees from Southeast Asia
8. Low-income and poor African Americans.

The changes that occurred after my arrival caused many of the long-term members to reconsider what they had envisioned and articulated as the congregation's future. They were forced to confront the fact that they had not conceived of the practical impact of their idealized vision. They had allowed me to implement a number of changes because they were so delighted and relieved to have a pastor on the job after two years without one. This rapid and multifaceted change disrupted the culture of the status quo. The growth of and change in the congregation also represented a challenge to the control of the long-term members. The new growth meant the possibility of a power shift. During the years following the rapid changes at First Church of God, there was a battle for dominance over vision, mission, and culture in the congregation.

I began to believe that my leadership was being sabotaged by some of the long-term members. The strategies of the status-quo leaders were executed at a subtle level. It is quite possible that the impulse to resist and reverse change had become an integral part of the congregational culture at First Church of God and occurred in an almost natural way. Some may not even have been aware that they were blocking change. I may have encountered time-honored methods of control and manipulation that had served the interests of the congregation's leadership for years. It is clear that I did not fully appreciate how radical the changes were that had been initiated. Naively, I had not planned for or expected resistance.

The process of seeking to transform an institution took a serious toll on my emotional health. I was unprepared for the stress that comes from pursuing institutional change. I now know that I also contributed to my own emotional state and the tensions in the congregation. I did not have a support network of pastors with which to share my concerns. I was not in regular contact with mentors. No one was attending to my emotional needs. And I was not seeking help to cope with the anxiety and exhaustion. I was not actively practicing spiritual disciplines of prayer, reflection, and the like. Nor had I prepared the congregation for a season of radical change. So some of their resistance was understandable.

On some mornings, in the solitude of my daily shower, I found myself weeping in response to the intense emotional pain of disillusionment and the weariness of exhaustion. I was completely spent emotionally and spiritually. During the last year or so of my pastorate, I sought the help of a therapist specially trained in assisting clergy. Then after nearly five years as the pastor of First Church of God, I resigned and left pastoral ministry. The chasm between First Church of God and Taco Bell Lutheran widened. Several of those who had joined First Church of God as a place of embrace and healing left as I did, disillusioned and searching.

✳✳✳

The story I have just recounted is my version and interpretation of the events that happened during my five years as a pastor at First Church of God in Minneapolis. Others who were there might view the circumstances differently. The point in retelling this episode in my life is to identify a question I struggle with: Do institutions help or hinder the process of rediscovering our humanity? I had arrived as the pastor of First Church of God full of hope and idealism regarding the potential of institutions to produce healthy environments for human development. I had high expectations for the possibility of institutional transformation—particularly in the context of the church.

When I left First Church of God, I was questioning my call to ministry, and I certainly wondered if the institutional church could be anymore than a place of dysfunction and pain. Where was that biblical community of love, reconciliation, and social justice? Where was the divine institution that the apostle Peter had called "a chosen race, a royal priesthood, a holy nation, God's own people" (1 Peter 2:9)? The idealism of the seminarian had been crushed after five years of serving in the institutional church.

I have seen glimmers of hope in each of the institutions I have participated in since leaving First Church of God. More often though, I have observed and experienced the politics of institutional life and its damaging effect on those who invest themselves in the organization's life. I have heard numerous stories of how people have felt abused and abandoned by institutions. Can organizations be places of care, concern, and compassion? While institutions are the way we organize community, national, or religious life to further shared agendas, they are also the primary vehicles in society for the reproduction of racism, sexism, and classism from one generation to the next. Perhaps the question is whether institutions can be redeemed. Can organizations produce healthy human community? Institutions are made up of people. So if individuals can become healthier, can the same happen in an organization when a group of people are on such a journey together?

Examples of congregations, organizations, and companies that build community, engender just relationships, and offer healing do exist. Yet these efforts are often successful only for a season, and then dysfunction enters the communal family or power needs emerge and cause division. Health and positive change in organizations are blocked by expediency, traditional ways of operation, denial of existing barriers, and the like. Rarely is sacrifice embraced and the focus placed on the needs of the whole rather than the individual.

I have direct experience with local congregations, denominations, nonprofit organizations, educational institutions, corporations, and grassroots movements. My experience with trying to develop healthy institutions has not been encouraging. I accept my share of the blame. I know that part of the responsibility for my lack of success has been my role—whether due to a lack of skill, patience, wisdom, or courage. But I ask again: Can institutions serve a redemptive purpose without also inflicting harm?

One of the ways institutions could become more diverse and reconciling is through empowering women and persons of color into positions of leadership with decision-making power. But I have learned that placing persons who have been marginalized or oppressed in society into positions of leadership does not by itself guarantee a more humane and just institution. It requires more than just changing top leadership. The entire institution must be transformed. Women can make decisions that continue to privilege men. People of color can make decisions that continue to privilege whites. A person's experience of discrimination does not ensure that he or she will lead in a more just fashion—or have the needed skill, determination, patience, wisdom, or courage to transform an institution. I have been disappointed by the actions of some social justice activists. I have observed situations where once they gain positions of leadership in organizations the feminist or the antiracist can reveal an elitist side.

I offer these thoughts with grace woven through them. As I reflect on my own involvement in institutions, I know I too have been infected by the dysfunction in the culture of the institutions I have sought to transform. This has caused me to behave at times in ways that mirrored the problem. I have provided leadership that failed to rise to the will of God. Institutions seem to multiply or magnify our individual sinfulness. Yes, I have been crushed by the dynamics of institutions. But I know that some who served in organizations in which I have provided leadership have experienced my actions as hurtful.

I continue to struggle with the role of institutions in our journey toward wholeness and humanity. While periodic signs of hope encourage me not to give up on the possibility that the answer can be affirmative, reality forces the query to remain in tension. As I get older, I become more pragmatic regarding institutional transformation. At the same time, I resist a debilitating cynicism. I still reach for hope, even if it is tempered by reality and girded with patience. And even when I have only hope because I believe in God—it is still hope. I see interplay between our own journey toward becoming healthy humans, our homecoming journey, and the work of humanizing our collective endeavors known as institutions. Making progress on our own homecoming journey toward rediscovering our humanity requires that we recognize in our fellow travelers the divine imprint of God. The more at home we feel in our own humanity—with our identity securely rooted in the fact that we are children of God—the more like home our institutions can become.

✻✻✻

After leaving First Church of God, I spent a year working on various projects. Then in 1991, I was selected as the first full-time staff person at Twin Cities Urban Resourcing Network (TURN). This presented me with a second opportunity to discover if organizations could contribute to the homecoming journey of making ourselves and our society healthier and more humane. This time I was not inheriting a fully developed organization like a church. TURN was launched in 1981 by a group of grassroots urban church leaders in Minneapolis and St. Paul who sought to empower a new generation of leaders from urban communities to heal the brokenness in the cities. That group soon called themselves the Twin Cities Urban Resourcing Network (TURN). For ten years TURN was an informal, volunteer-led city network comprised of leaders from urban congregations, nonprofit agencies, and the community, as well as some concerned suburban church leaders.

I was hired as the first executive director of TURN in 1991. During the early 1990s, the organization served as a catalyst for bringing together leaders from diverse cultures, races, social classes, and denominations who shared a common belief that faith is lived out through an active concern for the community. TURN advocated reconciliation, social justice, urban-suburban partnerships, community development, and the training of urban youth workers. At the core of TURN's work was a relational network. As TURN's only staff person, I was the primary networker—the relational glue that held the network together.

Therefore, much of my time was spent developing relationships. For example, when I first started working for TURN, I noticed that the network was primarily comprised of social justice-minded Evangelicals and Pentecostals interested in urban ministry. So I immediately focused my efforts on expanding the network. My Howard University degree opened doors to African American pastors in traditional black church denominations. My passion for social justice gave me the language to build relationships with mainline Protestant activists in the councils of churches. My days of daily Mass and intentional Franciscan community at Covenant House gave me a level of comfort in Roman Catholic settings.

During the first five years of my leadership at TURN, the organization was event driven. The events expanded the network. TURN had a knack for anticipating and responding to concerns in the community through catalytic events. I always told people that TURN was an organization with the feel of a movement. In the spring of 1992, TURN hosted a dialogue on racism and rage just a few days after the uprising in Los Angeles erupting from the Rodney King verdicts. More than seventy-five people squeezed into a monthly TURN dialogue that had been averaging twenty people. To our surprise Mayor Donald Frasier and City Council President Sharon Sayles Belton of Minneapolis were in attendance. Like a movement TURN could respond to events very quickly.

In the fall of 1992, I spoke at an interfaith community service of prayer for unity against violence where several hundred gathered from the Muslim, Jewish, and Christian communities in response to the killing of a police officer. My participation was the result of our networking. A few weeks later TURN sponsored the Bible in an Age of Multiculturalism conference, endorsed by the historically black denomination the National Baptist Convention of Minnesota and the councils of churches in Minneapolis and St. Paul. Over 250 people (equally divided among whites and persons of color) attended this event, held at the historic Pilgrim Missionary Baptist Church in St. Paul and featuring Cain Hope Felder and Cheryl Sanders. Like a movement TURN was in the mix on social issues that mattered.

In 1994, TURN cosponsored with the Chicago-based Seminary Consortium on Urban Pastoral Education (SCUPE) an event called The Fear Within that Breeds the Violence Without, with James Forbes as the keynote speaker. The instincts of the TURN network somehow sensed what was approaching. The following year Minneapolis set a new homicide record and was dubbed by the national press, "Murderapolis." Like a movement TURN was ahead of the trends.

In the aftermath of the O.J. Simpson trial verdicts, TURN joined with the Greater Minneapolis Council of Churches and other church leaders to bring together five hundred people, nearly evenly divided among African Americans and whites, wanting to bridge the divide of race, gender, class, and denomination. In 1996 TURN cohosted—with the Minnesota Council of Churches—the Call to Renewal antipoverty tour with Jim Wallis. Like a movement TURN was at the forefront of national concerns.

During the early 1990s, TURN events caused quite a stir. Through a series of public events and behind the scenes personal connections TURN became the glue for a relational network—a movement for positive social change and reconciliation in the Twin Cities. In the second half of the 1990s, TURN developed into a multi-staffed organization. TURN pursued its work through several collaborative partnerships. A number of program initiatives emerged out of these partnerships that provided resources for job training, urban youth development, volunteer placement, multicultural education, childcare, and the equipping of pastors. The "R" in the TURN acronym was changed to "reconciliation," in order to reflect better the core of TURN's mission—Twin Cities Urban Reconciliation Network.

TURN grew from being a relational network of individual leaders to the organizational glue that held together institutional partnerships. As part of the McKnight Foundation's interfaith "Congregations in Community" initiative TURN mobilized faith-inspired volunteers to work in community-based organizations and urban churches serving children and families in poverty. In six years TURN placed over fifteen thousand volunteers. Other partnership programs emerged from these efforts at mobilizing volunteers. TURN provided over four hundred urban home-based childcare providers with start-up packages, offered soft skills training to nearly one hundred individuals moving from welfare to work, and hosted a management training program for urban pastors and Christian community leaders with more than seventy graduates in just over two years. TURN launched a Gifts in Kind (GIK) Distribution Center that, in my final year, gave away over one-million-dollars worth of donated new products for use in over one hundred local urban churches and ministries benefiting more than one hundred thousand people, as well as provided school products for over twenty-five thousand children in thirty-six St. Paul and Minneapolis city schools including children in homeless shelters. As I was leaving TURN in 2001, plans were underway to launch an urban youth initiative to train and fund youth pastors for urban congregations that had not been able to afford one. These programs were done through partnerships with government, NGOs, academic institutions, community-based nonprofits, churches, and foundations.

Side by side with the social service program initiatives, the feel of TURN as a movement continued. During the late 1990s, I served as the relational glue for pastors and community leaders in the Hawthorne and Jordan neighborhoods of Minneapolis. We established an ecumenical, neighborhood-based ministerial alliance for the purpose of empowering pastors to exercise their moral leadership, respond to the biblical call to be ministers of reconciliation, and offer healing in this community where their congregations were located. The Hawthorne and Jordan neighborhoods were experiencing very high rates of the symptoms of poverty—violence, drug trade, prostitution, and crime. Pastoral staffs from at least fifteen different congregations were full members of the alliance ranging from Pentecostal to Roman Catholic, nearly equally divided between African American and white. TURN's youth development specialist was even on loan to a multicultural congregation in the neighborhood.

The concept of "relational glue" summarizes the essence of my work for ten years at TURN, and it describes the actualization of the organization's mission. I was initially the relational glue for the TURN network, then for the TURN staff (as TURN itself became the organizational glue of several partnerships), and finally for the pastors in the Hawthorne-Jordan neighborhood. At the dawn of the twenty-first century, reconciliation had emerged as a primary focus of TURN's work in the Twin Cities through relational networking and the development of programs to serve that network.

I focused on reconciliation issues also within the internal structure of the organization of TURN. When I started at TURN in 1991, the board of directors had a token representation of people of color and women. By the end of 2001, TURN's board of directors was 90% persons of color. Three of the five board chairs during my tenure were women and four were persons of color. A board of directors that was predominately persons of color provided a balance of power in an organization committed to racial reconciliation but headed by a white. Women board chairs provided a balance of power in an organization committed to gender justice but headed by a male. I started in 1991 as a solo white male staff person. By the end of 2001, TURN had eighteen full- and part-time staff members. The staff was 30% persons of color and predominately women.

With all of the success and changed lives in the public arena of TURN's work, the internal institutional dynamics did not consistently reflect reconciliation. At times the staff experienced disunity and dysfunctional organizational culture. We struggled internally with race, gender, and class tensions. TURN facilitated reconciliation in the public arena but sometimes struggled to live this reality as a staff. I believe that some of the responsibility for this tension between public work and private experience was a result of my personality and leadership style. I was the relational glue for the staff but I did not develop the quality of direct relationships needed among individual staff members. So even though I had good relationships with most of the staff, I did not translate these staff relationships into a functioning team. I also preferred to avoid conflict. When there was relational tension, I would negotiate and finesse the individual relationships I had with each staff member rather than bring individuals face to face with each other.

I also made some erroneous assumptions about us. I believed that most of the staff members were committed to and completely understood reconciliation. Over time it became clear that we had good intentions but did not always fully embrace or promote a reconciliation worldview. We as a staff were not that different from the society we were trying to serve as a healing balm. We needed to mature in our understanding and practice of reconciliation. We looked good as an organization and did the right things publicly, but sometimes failed internally.

Like at First Church of God, I began to experience seasons of discouragement and burnout. In retrospect, I now believe that I was not equipped with all of the skills and competence necessary to lead a staffed organization. I was sometimes in over my head. So emotional burnout was an expected result. This is not an excuse for my failures in leadership. I certainly could have made other choices or sought coaching for my lack of knowledge and experience. I do not accept all of the blame for TURN's moments of internal dissonance. Some of it was the reality of our organizational life and structure. Movement-like organizations often do not take the time needed to do internal work. Causes always need to be addressed immediately. Organizations believe that the issues they are addressing in society are far more important than the inner workings that lead to organizational health. Internal institutional transformation requires so much more emotionally from the leadership than public efforts at social change. The push for funding in nonprofit organizations often determines direction, defeats idealism, and limits the time necessary for internal dialogue.

My five years at First Church of God and my ten years at TURN left me confused and dispirited. I was unable to transform and heal the internal dysfunction that eventually led to collapse. First Church of God declined in members after I left, soon becoming a smaller congregation than when I arrived. Following my departure TURN changed direction, became a smaller organization, and then ceased to exist due to a lack of funding. Can organizations really be healthy?

Perhaps I should be content with the positive work of serving the community and meeting the needs of many people. I moved these organizations toward a public witness to reconciliation and social justice. Maybe that is the best that can be expected from these imperfect vehicles called institutions. First Church of God touched the lives of many individuals helping them get through life from one week to the next. Some of the folks in that small congregation have emerged as national leaders in addressing poverty, domestic abuse, sexism, and racism. TURN served the Twin Cities for many years as a reconciliation network bridging some very wide gaps across culture, socioeconomic class, gender, religion, and the like. Former staff members of TURN and members of the network continue to pursue the vision and witness that provided the impetus for TURN's impact. They are leaders locally, nationally, and internationally.

But I cannot let go of the notion that people working inside of institutions committed to reconciliation and social change should also be experiencing that reality in their organizational lives together. Organizations working for healthy communities ought to be healthy themselves. The communal life fostered around the table at Taco Bell Lutheran appears a lot simpler. Perhaps that gathering of people who were struggling to address their own personal demons of dysfunction had learned something profound. Their transparent discussions about religion and real life encouraged a lot of love and care for each other. Maybe it is that simple.

Roots in Roxbury

A few months prior to my fiftieth birthday, my mother sent me an email that included this notation:

> Thomas Bedonah, a negro man belonging to Roxbury and Lydia his wife, formerly Lydia Crafts, an English-woman,' presented for fornication before marriage, 1704. –*Court of Sessions of the Peace*, 1702–12, p. 32.[1]

My mother had been studying the genealogy of her family and discovered that we have an ancestor named Thomas Bedoona who was black (Bedonah is an alternate spelling). My immediate response was to smile. My life has been significantly shaped by living in and working with communities of color, particularly in regard to the African American community. All this time I was unaware that I had a black ancestor.

Julia Bedunah was my mother's grandmother. My ancestors after Thomas Bedoona spelled their surname "Bedunah." (In historical records regarding Thomas Bedoona, one also finds the name spelled Bedonah, Baduna, Badoona, and Bedouna. There may not have been a standard written form.) So from Thomas to me the generations are as follows: Thomas Bedoona—Ebenezer Bedunah—Moses Bedunah—John Bedunah—Moses Bedunah—George Bedunah—Julia Bedunah—Ned Curtiss—Marylin Curtiss (my mother)—Curtiss DeYoung. I am nine generations down the line from Thomas Bedoona. His wife, Lydia Craft, was the granddaughter of Lieutenant Griffin Craft, one of the founders of Roxbury, Massachusetts. Griffin

Craft arrived in Massachusetts from England in 1630 sailing on the Arabella with John Winthrop's fleet. Lydia's father, John Craft, was the first recorded birth in the town of Roxbury. Frances S. Drake noted in his book *The Town of Roxbury*, "Griffin Craft, the founder of this family in New England, was perhaps the first white settler in Roxbury."[2] Griffin held several positions of leadership in Roxbury and was one of the founders of the First Church in Roxbury where Thomas Weld served as the first pastor and John Eliot was ordained.

The exact date for the birth of Thomas Bedoona is not known. In Mormon church genealogical records it is listed variously from 1677–1680, with the majority of citations giving the 1680 date. Lydia Craft was born in 1681. They are both listed as born in Roxbury. The earliest historical reference to Thomas Bedoona that I have found is a listing of his marriage to Lydia Craft on October 4, 1703, in *A Report of the Record Commissioners of the City of Boston*. Judge Samuel Sewall officiated at their marriage ceremony.[3] Judge Sewall was one of the few, if only, public voices speaking out against slavery during this time. Three years prior to the marriage of Thomas and Lydia, Sewall wrote a public essay of protest against slavery in New England.[4] Thomas and Lydia Bedoona had seven children. Thomas Bedoona died on March 31, 1733, in Roxbury. The inventory of Thomas' estate, prepared by his widow Lydia, noted that he owned a house on eight acres of land with a barn, orchards, and some cows. Thomas Bedoona was listed as a husbandman, that is, a farmer.[5]

Blacks arrived in Massachusetts in the late 1620s or early 1630s. By 1680, when Thomas was born, there were fewer than two hundred blacks living in the colony of Massachusetts.[6] That number increased to five hundred and fifty by 1708.[7] Only a few blacks lived in Roxbury during this time. Twenty years after Thomas Bedoona's death, the 1754–1755 census recorded only fifty-three blacks living in Roxbury.[8]

Thomas Bedoona was born during a brief time in the history of colonial America when racial categories and life opportunities were not fixed. Racial prejudice was still very common. Most whites embraced the idea that blacks were inferior to whites and bore the curse of Ham. But in seventeenth-century Massachusetts, blacks and whites received very similar treatment under the law. The Puritans in Massachusetts believed that justice was universal and needed to be delivered in a fair and equal fashion. For instance, in the case of the crime of fornication, with which Thomas and Lydia were charged, whites and blacks received equal punishment. Both blacks and whites could own property. As I noted, Thomas Bedoona was a land owner.[9]

These sentiments started to change in the 1680s, when laws focusing on the behavior of servants were passed, such as limitations on alcohol use. The introduction of a master-servant divide in the law meant that Massachusetts society began to move away from fairness as a guiding principle. This shift affected all servants, whether black, white, or Native American. It was not long until these legal and social changes were racialized. In 1703 a 9:00 pm curfew was declared for black and Native American servants and slaves.[10]

The first law against interracial marriage in Colonial America was passed in 1664 in Maryland. In 1697 the Massachusetts Bay assembly dictated that blacks who committed fornication with an English person should be whipped. (I do not know if Thomas and Lydia were found guilty of the fornication charges against them.) Two years after the 1703 marriage of the Bedoonas, a law was passed in Massachusetts against sexual intercourse and marriage between the races. Thomas was just a step ahead of a society's embrace of a legalized racism and a permanent system of chattel slavery based on race.[11]

I do not know the status of Thomas Bedoona. Since he married a white Englishwoman from a prominent Roxbury family and owned his own home, I assume that at least by adulthood Thomas was a free black man. I have no information on Thomas' parents. Regarding the children of couples like Thomas and Lydia, Lorenzo Green writes, "By the common law of England, which prevailed in the colonies, children held the same status as the father. In essence, the child was free or slave, depending on the condition of the father."[12] Since there is no record of the Bedoona children being slaves, Thomas must have been free. Kevin Mumford notes that in interracial relationships during that time, the children followed "the condition" of the mother.[13] The Bedoona children must have been considered ethnically and racially white, since their mother's condition was that of a white Englishwoman.

The white status of the Bedoona children was even more probable given the fact that they grew up during a time when interracial marriage was illegal. If they had been considered black, they would have been required to marry persons who were black. This explains how and why the Bedunahs in the United States were and are considered white. Eventually, the "blackness" or "African-ness" of Thomas Bedoona and his descendants disappeared from the family's stories and known historical documents. The truth remained hidden in an obscure historical record, which declared that Thomas was a "Negro." Lydia's English heritage trumped Thomas' "Negro" heritage in racist colonial America (and even more so in the soon to be new nation of the United States). This is how I could be nearly fifty years old before I first learned that I have black ancestry. Many of my ancestors never knew their full heritage.

The origins of Thomas Bedoona are presently unknown. He appears in the history and genealogies without any record of parents or home of origin or even an exact birth date. I do not know if Thomas was born a slave, an indentured servant, or a free person. I do not know if his parents arrived in North

America directly from Africa, the Caribbean islands, or were themselves born slaves, indentured servants, or free persons. One obvious theory for the relationship between Thomas and Lydia would be that Thomas was a slave of the Crafts family and became involved with Lydia through this contact. There is no record of this, and it seems that no one in the Crafts family was a slave owner until after the death of Thomas Bedoona. It is interesting to note that family patriarch Griffin Craft's great-grandson Deacon Ebenezer Craft did own black slaves in Roxbury. Living during that same period of history was another great-grandson of Lieutenant Craft, Thomas and Lydia's mixed race son (and my ancestor) Ebenezer Bedunah. Like Deacon Craft, he was also a church member. This conjures up a troubling image of a biracial Ebenezer and his slave-owning cousin Ebenezer praying together at family gatherings.[14]

When I shared the news about my black ancestor with friends, responses varied. My African American friends said things like: "Welcome to the family brother," "I am not surprised there is *blood* in your blood," "This explains everything. I always knew deep down you were a brother!" Even my wife joked, "How interesting! So I'm married to a black man." Interestingly, few of my white friends commented. My students at Bethel University, particularly the students of color, enjoyed the revelation and made quite a big deal of it for some weeks. Word of my new "status" spread quickly among other students of color at Bethel University, and it was big news.

These responses were predicated on the way blackness has been historically defined in the United States. Many states had laws that determined one's race based on a percentage of "Negro" ancestry. Eventually most states in the United States either legally defined or socially practiced what came to be known as the "one drop rule." If a person had at least one drop of African blood running through her or his veins, that person was classified as black. Some states used the language "any discernable trace" of Negro heritage. Under the "one drop rule," my discovery of a black ancestor makes me black (even though I am only about .2% or $1/512^{th}$ of African descent).

A discovery like this prior to the mid-1960s, in much of the United States, would have changed my racial status from white to black. This change in status would have affected my job opportunities, where I could live, my social relationships, and my experience of racial bigotry. I surmised that in the early eighteenth century the children of Thomas and Lydia Bedoona, with half of their ancestry black African, were declared white. In the twentieth century, with 99.8% of my heritage white European, I could have been classified as black. The Bedoona children and their descendents lost the truth of their identity, and I have just rediscovered mine. The politics of race and identity are ridiculous, confusing, devious, mysterious, and troubling—all at the same time. I presently identify myself as a white male of Dutch and English ancestry with one drop of African blood who is a citizen of the United States. Even though I fully embrace and rejoice in my black African ancestry, in the twenty-first century "one drop" has not changed the fact that I am a person with race, class, and male privilege.

Traveling through the complexities of race and identity from Harlem back in history to Roxbury has been a life-changing journey. On this homecoming journey I have experienced my humanity in new and healing ways at a church in Harlem, connected to a lineage of mentors that have guided my path with wisdom, sought to reconcile my white male privilege with a rage against racism, encountered an authentic sense of community at Taco Bell, and discovered a long lost truth about a black African ancestor. And this is only the first part of my story of homecoming.

Part Two
Johannesburg to Jerusalem
The Intersection of Global Cultures and Religious Faiths

❋

Thus far I have reflected on my journey within the confines of the United States—and colonial America—from Harlem to Roxbury. These boundaries kept me focused on my experiences as a "white" male seeking to resist the allure of privilege while navigating a role of solidarity with those negatively affected by injustices and the racialization of society.

Now I share about my journeys in the global arena. My first trip overseas was to attend a conference in Salzburg, Austria, in 1999. This event opened my life to a whole new adventure. I came face to face with a wide range of cultural expressions and religious diversity. The human family became bigger, as did my understanding of God. My understanding of homecoming expanded as the places I call home multiplied. The quiet voice of divine expectation was heard again as I took a journey through the intersection of global cultures and religious faiths. This path took me through Johannesburg in South Africa and on to the Holy City of Jerusalem.

CHAPTER FIVE

A Global Faith

I sat in the audience engaged by the remarks of Bishop Samuel Ruiz Garcia from Chiapas, Mexico. Bishop Ruiz was a founder and champion of Latin American liberation theology and a nominee for the Nobel Peace Prize. He spoke eloquently and with a pastoral spirit about the relationship of religion to race and ethnicity. Following his presentation I was stunned at how audience members angrily bombarded this passionate spokesperson for the liberation of the poor. A barrage of questions shot forth regarding the church's complicity with injustice and oppression around the world. Many of those gathered had direct experience with religious institutions that behaved in ways that betrayed any commitment to liberation or social justice. They had seen firsthand the hypocrisy of religious leaders.

Rather than reacting defensively, the bishop responded with grace and diplomacy, acknowledging the many ways the institutional church had failed. Then he said, in essence, "But I am not speaking about a church against the poor or even a church for the poor. I am speaking about a church *of* the poor." In the opening session of the October 1999 Salzburg Seminar, Bishop Ruiz redefined true religion as an authentically *lived* faith in God.

It was a rare and distinct honor to be selected as a McKnight Foundation Fellow for the 1999 Salzburg Seminar, "Race and Ethnicity: Social Change through Public Awareness." More than seventy people from nearly forty nations gathered to consider the challenges facing our world regarding race and ethnicity. Never have I enjoyed such an opportunity as this to address issues I feel so strongly about in what amounted to a weeklong event reminiscent of the United Nations.

The Salzburg Seminar began after World War II, in 1947, as a safe place for intellectuals from Europe, both East and West, and the United States to discuss a wide range of issues. The tensions between the Soviet Union-Eastern Europe and the United States-Western Europe were a primary focus. The Salzburg Seminar expanded to a truly international think tank tackling global issues after the demise of communism in Europe. The speakers and fellows through the years have included a host of important leaders from Africa, Asia, Europe, and the Americas—Kofi Annan, Ralph Ellison, Vaclav Havel, Margaret Mead, John Hope Franklin, and several United States Supreme Court justices. The Salzburg Seminar is convened at Schloss Leopoldskron, a historic estate best known in the United States as the backdrop for the 1965 movie "The Sound of Music." The city of Salzburg sits in the Austrian Alps and combines the beauty of the mountains with old European architecture. Salzburg is also the birthplace of the musical genius Wolfgang Amadeus Mozart.

The Salzburg Seminar had sponsored a weeklong event two years earlier with a similar group of individuals on the subject of cultural diversity. According to Salzburg Seminar staff, that week had disintegrated into chaos and animosity as people debated whose oppression and suffering ranked as the most tragic. Bishop Ruiz set a different tone that permeated our discussions and the ways we engaged with each other during the week. Our spirits became more unified as we chose to pursue positive outcomes rather than wallow in the negative. We did acknowledge and process the pain and suffering, but we responded with hope and creative thinking.

Others built on the bishop's foundational opening remarks. Ronald Takaki, a professor at the University of California, Berkeley, presented a way to look at history from a multicultural perspective. He illustrated how intertwined are the histories of the indigenous peoples of North America and the various groups of people who have settled in the United States through immigration, refugee resettlement, and slavery. Yet he acknowledged how often this history has been suppressed and controlled by a powerful elite in order to protect and promulgate a "master narrative." Giving words to the tone set by Bishop Ruiz, Professor Takaki asked the group to struggle with the question: "What are the ties that bind? What are the ties that can bind a racially and ethnically diverse people into one people?"

Yasmin Alibhai-Brown, a journalist from Great Britain, identified herself as British from Asian (India) ancestry and Muslim. She shared about the challenge of confronting injustice in the government and police through her weekly newspaper column. Every Thursday her column appeared in *The Independent*. Many Fridays she received hate mail and death threats. She closed her remarks by referring to Ronald Takaki's question about the "ties that bind." Yasmin Alibhai-Brown asked us to consider what we needed to sacrifice to discover ties that bind?

Civil rights lawyer and Professor Lani Guinier, from Harvard University, offered a provocative lecture on "the miner's canary." In the coalmine a canary is sent ahead of the miners to detect poisonous fumes. If the canary gets sick or dies, the miners leave the mine. As persons who experience injustice and prejudice, Guinier suggested that people of color and women serve a similar role to the miner's canary in the United States. If we want to address injustice, we need to listen to miner's canaries in our societies as they identify oppression in its many forms. Following her lecture I asked how we ensure that the canaries—persons experiencing oppression—are not critically harmed by the fumes of injustice. I also suggested that white males need to acquire some canary senses so that they too can recognize injustice.

The final three presenters moved us out of the world of concepts to the streets of real life. South African Njabulo Ndebele, a noted author of fiction and poetry, a social critic, and a leader in higher education spoke about how language influences our understanding of race and ethnicity. South Africa has eleven official languages. Dr. Ndebele noted how language is closely tied to identity. Your "identity" affects your access to opportunities. The ability to speak several languages in South Africa provides entrée. Dr. Helen Kivnick, a psychologist and professor of social work at the University of Minnesota, demonstrated the power of music in sustaining efforts at social change and as an instrument of social change. Shyam Benegal, who has been at the forefront of making feature films in India, spoke of the possibilities and limitations of using film to create public awareness for social change.

Conversations with presenters and with other participants (most of whose credentials qualified them to be lecturers) were amazing experiences in stimulating international dialogue. The assembled group represented a wide array of freedom fighters, academics, directors of nonprofits, advisors to presidents and prime ministers, providers of mass media, and grassroots activists. In the course of informal conversations, I heard stories told by former freedom fighters from the Czech Republic, South Africa, and Ethiopia. I spoke with an academic from China who was one of a very small number of individuals in his country of over a billion people examining race and ethnicity from a non-Marxist perspective. My week at the Salzburg Seminar certainly expanded my world and my worldview.

Prior to my experience at the Salzburg Seminar, I felt little compulsion to expand my perspective and work beyond the urban centers of the United States. I would tell people that my calling was to the city in domestic settings. I rarely gave a second thought to international opportunities. If my trip to the Salzburg Seminar was not such an honor and had not been fully funded by the McKnight Foundation, I probably would have passed on the offer. The experience at the Salzburg Seminar, followed by ten days in Amsterdam and Paris with my family, caused a radical shift in my psyche from an exclusively domestic calling to a global commitment.

The setting of the Salzburg Seminar also affected how I understood my faith and the religious faith of others. When we introduced ourselves the first night, I followed the lead of a Presbyterian pastor (the only other clergy person in attendance except for the bishop) and mentioned that I was an ordained minister. After hearing the angry questions that Bishop Ruiz received, I questioned the wisdom in sharing with the group my clergy status. It was too late. I had identified myself as a Christian. And even worse, as an ordained minister I was part of the institutional church. A few of those in attendance took full advantage of the opportunity to share with me their horror stories from church involvement. I listened compassionately and affirmed the unfortunate reality of their complaints.

Following the bishop's lead, I also discovered that my faith had to be expressed through actions and attitudes rather than words. So I commenced to witness through *being* a follower of Jesus and spoke of my personal faith only when invited. It was of little help to appeal to the New Testament in this setting where Hindus and Jews came from religious traditions with scriptures more ancient than mine, and Muslims held to the authority of the Qur'an. My only authority came from living my faith—much like what was required of first-century Christians. Perhaps that is what Jesus had in mind when he spoke to his disciples that last time, "You will be my witnesses in Jerusalem, and in all Judea and Samaria, and to the ends of the earth" (Acts 1:8b).

✳✳✳

This was not my first involvement in interfaith settings. Nearly ten years earlier, I had prepared a report on the faith community in Milwaukee, Wisconsin, that involved me interviewing eighty religious leaders from many faith groups including Christianity, Judaism, Islam, Buddhism, Bahai, and the Native American Church.[1] Also my work at TURN led me to the McKnight Foundation project, eventually named "Congregations in Community," which was designed by a group of us from the Christian, Jewish, and Muslim faith communities five years prior to my visit to Salzburg. I spent many hours sitting with a Rabbi, an Imam, and two other Christian clergy as we learned how we could work and dream together in order to address poverty through faith-inspired volunteerism. Yet these relationships occurred in Christian dominated settings. The Salzburg Seminar offered the experience of a plurality of perspectives with no single religion dominating. The week in Salzburg took me farther than I had anticipated down the path of interfaith understanding. While I learned some extremely valuable lessons in how to live in a world where people practice many different faiths or even hold a cynicism regarding religion, I also grew in my respect for and value of other faith traditions.

An emotionally moving event during that week at the Salzburg Seminar provides an illustration. Elections had occurred the week prior to our arrival in Austria. The political party that finished second in the election voting was influenced by neo-Nazi ideology. I also learned that during World War II the Nazis occupied Schloss Leopoldskron where we met each day. On the final evening of the seminar, an impromptu religious service was led by Jewish participants to welcome the

Sabbath—in this building where Nazi SS officers were once trained and in a country that was experiencing the reemergence of anti-Semitism. It was a poignant and holy moment, and I felt the presence of God.

It would be several years before I would again feel the presence of God in another religious milieu. In January 2006, I traveled to Thailand and Egypt. I prepared for the trip by reading about Buddhism, Islam, and the lives of the founders, Buddha and Muhammad. I first stopped for five days in Chiang Mai, Thailand. I enjoyed the warm weather, the delightful Thai food, and the cultural diversity. I had the opportunity to visit many Buddhist Wats (temples). The architecture was quite beautiful. I was also inspired by the sincerity and commitment of the people who came for worship. The most spectacular temple that I visited sat on top of a 5,283 foot mountain. Wat Phra That Doi Suthep is considered one of the four most important temples in Thailand.

One day I sat in the Wat Phra Singh in the center of the city of Chiang Mai. In front of me was a large golden Buddha casting his eyes over the entire sanctuary. To my left was a solitary monk chanting and receiving gifts from the faithful. Many people bowed, greeted the Buddha, and kissed the floor. This ritual was not all that different from the genuflection in Catholicism acknowledging the eucharistic host. After ten or fifteen minutes of observation, I moved to a side sanctuary, the Viharn Laikam, which housed the early image of Buddha, the Phra Buddha Singh. As I entered the building, a group of monks were chanting. It was a beautiful and soothing sound much like Gregorian chant. I found it to be quite a worshipful experience. Unfortunately, modern technology interrupted the sacred moment. A worshiper sitting down front, a few feet from the monks, had forgotten to turn off her cell phone. When the phone rang, the ring tone was, "Jingle Bells." The monks continued to chant while "Jingle

Bells" provided a counter melody to their splendid melodic chants. I suppose the human element interrupts all religions. I must admit that, as much as I tried, I never did fully understand Buddhism. The "Jingle Bells" interruption symbolized my attempts to find God in Buddhist Wats. My strong monotheistic faith orientation kept interrupting my efforts to experience Buddhism.

Next I traveled to Egypt. While in Cairo I went to a mosque for Friday noon prayers. The men gathered in the mosque and spilled out into the streets, which had been blocked off and covered with prayer mats. We all removed our shoes on the prayer mats. As men arrived they would bow, kneel, and offer some personal prayers. The liturgy of Islam had a familiarity to it for a Christian. The service began with a call to prayer— a melodic chant reciting verses from the Qur'an over a loud speaker. I am sure at some point in the service they prayed the opening lines of the Qur'an: "In the name of God, the Lord of Mercy, the Giver of Mercy! Praise belongs to God, Lord of the Worlds, the Lord of Mercy, the Giver of Mercy, Master of the Day of Judgment. It is You we worship; it is You we ask for help. Guide us to the straight path: the path of those You have blessed, those who incur no anger and who have not gone astray" (sura 1). Next was a sermon. The entire service was in Arabic. People sat next to each other across all socio-economic class, ethnic, and occupational lines. I saw a well dressed man of some means sitting next to a sanitation worker in his soiled work clothes.

The service ended with communal prayer, a unison reciting of prayers. The men stood side by side in lines across. If there was an empty space in the line one is beckoned forward to fill the space. At this point I was invited into the line. So I observed the men near me to know what to do—when to bow and kneel. It was quite impressive to see the dedication of those in attendance. As we bowed and then got down on our

knees and placed our face to the ground, I felt myself spiritually engaged by the moment of prayer. I felt as though I was
in the presence of God. It was frustrating not to know Arabic.
So my prayers used the Christian religious language of my
own devotional life.

Not only did the Salzburg Seminar place me in the midst of
several religious perspectives, it was the most diverse multicultural and international experience of my life. I was stretched
in so many ways as I moved from conversations with South
Africans, to Chinese, to Czechs, to Ethiopians, to Mexicans,
to Nepalese, to Palestinians, to Israelis, to Guatemalans, to
Spaniards, and on and on. All of this stretching took place in
Salzburg, Austria. The effect of a cultural expanse became
even more real with the move from Chiang Mai to Cairo. For
the first time in my life, I moved directly from one unfamiliar
culture to another. This was very disorienting due to the mas-
sive cultural shift: Asia to Africa, Thai to Arabic, Buddhism to
Islam, a city of two million to an urban metropolis of twenty
million, and a seven hour time shift (after a fifteen-hour time
shift from Minnesota to Thailand). When I arrived in Cairo, I
felt almost dizzy. I had no anchor to secure me in this fluidity
of cultural images and settings.

Just about the time I had gained my cultural footing in
Cairo, I embarked on a train ride to Aswan in the southern
part of Egypt. For my comfort and safety, I was told that I
would ride in the tourist car rather than the one used by most
average Egyptians. When I stepped into the train, I discovered
that my ticket did not place me in the tourist car as I expected.
I was the only non-Egyptian in my train car for an overnight
journey of thirteen hours. I felt so all alone and nervous on
a very noisy and crowded train ride with families and crying
babies. Some of the travelers were dressed in their Islamic
garb. One couple that sat close to me was clothed all in black
and the wife's hijab completely covered her face with only slits

for her eyes to see out. It took all of my prayers and whatever composure I could muster not to be overcome with fear from horribly negative stereotypes of Islamic terrorists.

I had timed my trip so that after thirteen hours of travel I would know that I had arrived at the stop for Aswan and I would get off of the train. That plan was disrupted when the train just stopped on the tracks and sat for an hour and made a few other unscheduled stops. Now I had no idea what time we would arrive in Aswan. As we got closer to my final destination, I realized that all of the signs were in Arabic. How would I know when and where to get off? Finally, I did locate an English speaker and confirmed my point of departure from the train. The return trip was a repeat of the experience. The man from the tour office spoke little English and tried to explain to me some confusion with the tickets. I just hoped I had what I needed. This whole drama caused the professor of reconciliation to feel extremely uncomfortable and culturally stretched.

Entering the cultural and religious space of others is a bold act. Often it is very uncomfortable, lonely, and stressful. But I have always found it eventually enriching, engaging, and invigorating. I have found friends and kindred spirits in many cultural and religious settings. I have learned that the human family is much bigger and more diverse than I can imagine. Sometimes I find that I have more in common with social justice and peace activists from other cultures and religious faiths than I do with Christians from the United States. I have also discovered that God is much bigger than most of us believe or experience. I have experienced God in a Jewish ritual and at an Islamic mosque, as well as in Harlem, Times Square, Washington, Johannesburg, Guatemala City, Chang Mai, Salzburg, Jerusalem, and at Taco Bell Lutheran.

❈❈❈

When I attempted to describe the week at the Salzburg Seminar to friends and colleagues after returning home, I was told I spoke with great passion and had a "glow" about me. Some asked if the experience of the seminar caused me to move in a new direction in life. One ministry friend asked if my "call" had changed. It took several weeks to disengage from the experience of the Salzburg Seminar. I kept ruminating on what transpired during that week together with so many people whose perspectives both challenged and enriched my own. For several weeks I felt as though I was still walking—intellectually, emotionally, and spiritually—through the halls of Schloss Leopoldskron in Salzburg. I had experienced a sense of homecoming in this world house. This was a pivotal moment in my life and leadership.

As I write now, I realize that this week was another moment of divine expectation—"to whom much is given, much is expected." The divine expectation emerging from a week in Salzburg, Austria, demanded that I seek to understand life from a viewpoint that considers all of the ways we express our humanity across this earth. I also must ask myself: What does all this mean for someone pursuing the ministry of reconciliation? As Ronald Takaki said at the Salzburg Seminar: "What are the ties that bind?" Even now nearly ten years later, I have not made full sense of that week in Salzburg, Austria. I continue to unpack the meaning found in that extraordinary event. I do know this much: I must integrate this intense experience into my life, work, faith, value system, hopes, and vision of the world. As a result of attending the Salzburg Seminar, I now reflect on issues from a vantage point that embraces the broad multicultural, international, multilingual, interfaith, multi-perspective context of our world. After Salzburg my world had grown. I became a world citizen with a global faith.

CHAPTER SIX

The Jesus Was Black Tour

Six years after the 1994 elections that brought Nelson Mandela to the presidency, I found myself in the country of South Africa and on the continent of Africa for the first time. I was invited by two South Africans who had been at the Salzburg Seminar to present a four-day workshop titled "The Bible and Culture in the Twenty-First Century" at a national conference for youth leaders. Individuals from all four racial groups as defined under apartheid were in attendance: black indigenous Africans (from many ethnic groups), Coloureds (people of mixed race descent), Indians (originally from India), and whites (Afrikaans- and English-speaking). In the first session we examined the multiculturalism of the Bible.

Equipped with maps and biblical references, I detailed what has been rediscovered and documented by many biblical scholars of color including my mentor Cain Hope Felder. The Bible begins in Genesis with one race, the human race. Four rivers surrounded the Garden of Eden—two from the continent of Asia and two from the continent of Africa. Black people are not cursed as descendants of Ham as some have claimed, because Ham was never cursed. Nor are blacks the cursed descendants of Cain. Cain was not cursed. (Also, according to the Bible none of his descendants survived the flood.) People and places from the continent of Africa are mentioned over 850 times in the Bible. There is an extensive

Asian presence in the Scriptures. The biblical Hebrews were a multicultural, multiracial people with a lineage rooted in both Asia and Africa and an identity shaped by their faith rather than their race.

To my amazement the people who gathered in my workshop had never heard this information before. Here we were on the continent of Africa and the extensive presence of Africans in the Bible was unknown. A church leader proclaimed, "I am finally able to say that I am proud to be both black and a Christian!" A youth worker from the township of Soweto stated, "I have always connected to my faith in God through a relationship with a living Christ, not through the Bible. Discovering that there are Africans in the Bible is empowering. Christianity is not the white man's religion!"

On the second day, I described how white images became the dominant and exclusive representation of Jesus Christ in every part of the world. I spoke of how the domination of these white images, during the last several centuries, damaged and sabotaged the potential to transform people's lives—particularly in regions populated by persons of color. Then we discussed the racial and cultural heritage of the historic Jesus of Nazareth. I shared that many scholars now speak of Jesus as an Afro-Asiatic Jew. This again was a new revelation. All of the participants had accepted that Jesus was a white European because of the white images they had observed since childhood.

This new awareness sparked quite a discussion. The black indigenous Africans were ready to embrace a black African Jesus. The Indians announced the fact that Jesus was an Asian. The Coloureds took note that Jesus was Afro-Asiatic, therefore multiracial. So they spoke of a Coloured Jesus. Some of the whites in the session acknowledged that whites had "owned" the image of Jesus for far too long, and they were willing to accept these new understandings as part of the hope for the

future of a new church for a new South Africa. This knowledge was empowering and liberating.

I was invited to return to the same conference in 2002 as
the plenary speaker. This time my entire family traveled with
me. As was the case in 2000, a few hundred youth leaders,
youth workers, and youth pastors attended. They came fresh
from settings where youth faced the challenges of poverty, violence, HIV/AIDS, and racism. The attendees were from all of
the racial and cultural groups represented in South Africa, as
well as from neighboring countries like Swaziland, Botswana,
Lesotho, Zimbabwe, Namibia, and Zambia. Once more I
offered my workshop on the multiculturalism of the Bible.
The dialogue that ensued in these sessions, and in subsequent
conversations, revealed again the liberating power of truth. In
the final session of the workshop in 2002, I asked each individual to send a video greeting to people in the United States.
One black leader who had also been at the workshop in 2000
gave his greeting. Then he pointed at the camera and said,
"And Jesus is Black!" South Africans of different races, as well
as other Africans in the workshop, repeated this litany.

My third visit to South Africa was a speaking tour. My invitation to speak came from several people who attended workshops I presented in 2000 and 2002. The name for this 2003
speaking tour echoed the refrain that ended the 2002 workshop—the "Jesus Was Black Tour." I knew that a provocative
title would draw attention, increase attendance, and produce
impassioned dialogue. The Jesus Was Black Tour took me to
four cities—Johannesburg, Cape Town, Port Elizabeth, and
Durban.

Johannesburg is large and cosmopolitan, the New York
City of South Africa. Most of my time was spent on the south
side where three communities of color, segregated from whites
and each other, were formed under the Group Areas Act of
the apartheid regime: Soweto, Lenasia, and Eldoradopark.

Soweto was reserved for indigenous black Africans, Lenasia for Indians, and Eldoradopark for Coloureds. The architects of apartheid went to great lengths to keep the races segregated. Soweto is the largest black township in South Africa. With a population estimated at several million, it sometimes is called Johannesburg's twin city. In June 1976 many children in Soweto were killed by the police in uprisings against the oppressive apartheid government.

South of Johannesburg and near the southernmost point of the continent lies Cape Town, a city of great natural beauty with two oceans and mountains that complement its thriving downtown and arts community. Right in the center of the city is the breathtaking Table Mountain. Some claim that Cape Town is the most beautiful city in the world. The dominant population is the Coloured mixed-race community. A very distinct Cape Town Coloured culture has developed with a jazz music tradition rivaling that in the United States. Cape Town is also the port where one takes the boat over to Robben Island, the island prison where Nelson Mandela spent nineteen of his twenty-seven years of incarceration in a small six-by-nine-foot cell.

Like Cape Town, Port Elizabeth is a beautiful city that sits on the Indian Ocean. Port Elizabeth is an unmistakably black African city. The architecture might have a European flavor, but the population and the culture are unapologetically black and Xhosa-speaking. Port Elizabeth is in the Eastern Cape—an area that produced many of the leaders of the anti-apartheid struggle, including Nelson Mandela.

Up the coast from Port Elizabeth is Durban, the second largest city in South Africa. Durban is on the Indian Ocean with a lovely beachfront similar to Port Elizabeth. It is very tropical and lush like Miami, Florida, except in Durban there are many hills. Culturally, Durban is Zulu and Indian. It is located in the province of KwaZulu-Natal where many Zulu people live. It is also home to one million Indians—the largest population of Indians outside of India. Both of these cultures affect and influence the feel of Durban.

Over the course of sixteen days on the Jesus Was Black Tour, I spoke nineteen times and participated in an additional twenty meetings, site visits, and media interviews. I spoke at churches, universities, faith-based organizations, and in homes. I spoke in formal and informal settings. My presentations ranged from twenty-minute messages to six-hour workshops. Speaking engagements and meetings were often added with short notice. The pace was hectic and exhilarating. I am normally a person who needs seven to eight hours of sleep. As an introvert I need times of reflection to regenerate. I did not have the luxury of much sleep or contemplation. Yet I did not feel their absence. Out of absolute necessity to depend on God, the Almighty provided all of the energy and insight that I needed.

The primary purpose of the Jesus Was Black Tour, like the workshops in 2000 and 2002, was to counter and dispel the belief that Christianity is an exclusive faith and to restore the biblical truth that people of all races and cultures are created fully in the image of God. This was the goal in all of my preaching, teaching, and dialoguing. The idea that Christianity is the white man's religion and the Bible is the white man's document still prevails. Yet Jesus of Nazareth was an Afro-Asiatic Jew. Furthermore, I noted that the proliferation of white images of Jesus and biblical characters has sabotaged the ability of the biblical message to be heard and embraced in many settings around the world. An exclusively "white" version of Christianity has been built on heretical notions and political agendas. This is in contrast to the Jesus in the Bible, who said he came to build "a house of prayer for all of the nations" (Mark 11:17).

In a few settings, the message seemed to be embraced without reservation. In Cape Town, I spoke to over one hundred students and faculty at Cornerstone Christian College. It appeared to me that most students were in their twenties and the crowd represented the diversity of South Africa. At the point in my message when I stated that Jesus was an Afro-Asiatic Jew, the students erupted in applause and started cheering in several languages. The white students clapped just as loudly. I have never had that happen when making such a pronouncement.

In most settings the response was mixed and intense dialogue occurred. But even in these settings, people shared how they felt liberated and empowered by the information I was presenting. The dialogue often heated up when discussing what to do about images of Jesus and the people of the Bible. Should we completely discard imagery, create new and diverse images, or seek to develop historic portrayals in regard to race and culture? I chose not to prescribe a response for the church in South Africa. I challenged leaders to address racism and replace it with truth and reconciliation in the church.

In my presentations I asked people to close their eyes and imagine Jesus walking toward them. Then I would ask them to describe what Jesus looked like. Most people saw a white man with northern European features. This particularly troubled persons of color. Some struggled with the notion that if humans were created in the image of God, and they as persons of color imagined Jesus as white, what did that say about their own sense of identity and worth? How could they overcome feelings of inferiority enforced and encouraged under apartheid with white images of Jesus Christ controlling their vision of the divine—and who was made in the image of God? Liberation occurred as individuals struggled to embrace freedom from this psychological and theological captivity.

I was told that after some sessions whites reported struggling with the notion of a Jesus that was black. Some said they could let go of a white image of Jesus but resisted the idea

of a black Jesus. The suggestion was that Jesus was neither
white nor black. Interestingly, I never asked anyone to accept
an exclusively black Jesus. I just pleaded that they reject the
notion of an exclusively white Jesus. I said that Jesus was an
Afro-Asiatic Jew—which in the United States does mean that
Jesus might be socially and culturally classified as black (at
least one drop of black African blood running through his
veins). Such resistance demonstrates how deep in the psyche
and how emotionally charged are beliefs about blackness as
a negative identity. I said in the presentations that, if we discovered a picture of Jesus of Nazareth that proved he was
black, our faith should not be affected. If we cannot easily
love, serve, and embrace a black Jesus, this reveals that our
faith is built on the race of Jesus and not on his death and
resurrection. One participant at a workshop told me that he
had heard a white person once say, "If Jesus is not white then
I am not a Christian."

For many young people the issue was truth. If the church
would lie about the color of Jesus, what else had the church
lied about? These presentations served to restore some integrity and credibility in the church through truth telling. On each
of my visits to South Africa, I have proclaimed that Jesus of
Nazareth was an Afro-Asiatic Jew. Therefore Jesus was a person of color—in South Africa that meant that Jesus was black
("black" in the vernacular of the liberation struggle included
all who faced the oppression of apartheid). I have proclaimed
this to whites from affluent Dutch Reformed Churches and to
persons who lived in squatter camps.

Preaching in South Africa that Jesus was black does not just
refer to skin color or only serve as a challenge to racism. Proclaiming that Jesus was black is also a prophetic word against
the great economic disparities in South Africa. Preaching the
blackness of Jesus means that he lives among the majority of
blacks in South Africa who experience powerlessness. I have

sensed the presence of this black Jesus when I walked the dusty roads that lead through informal settlements (squatter camps), sat in shacks with dirt floors and small rooms, and listened to mothers tell of the burdens of poverty, joblessness, and missing children. Yes, Jesus was there.

I also felt the presence of this black Jesus when I traveled in South African taxis—minivans filled beyond capacity (often sixteen people crammed into four bench seats). Most whites and many persons of color too refuse to ride in these taxis due to overcrowding, discomfort, and the poor condition of the vehicles. Yet this is the primary mode of transportation for poor and working class people. A black Jesus rides in taxis pressed on each side by the sweaty bodies of individuals who work hard every day cleaning and gardening at other people's homes.

A black Jesus was present at desperately poor township public schools. I particularly remember a high school where students lined up in the courtyard standing in close proximity to each other for the entire assembly. Yet their posture straightened with dignity when the music teacher led them in singing hymns in Xhosa. It seemed as though time stood still for a moment as the students sang with exquisite a cappella harmonies. The paradox of this beautiful music in the midst of such dehumanizing conditions was not lost on me. I imagine it was similar to the singing of angels heard by poor shepherds in Palestine the night that Jesus was born in the unsanitary conditions of a barn and laid in a saliva-drenched, animal-feeding trough to serve as his crib. Perhaps the singing by these students served as an antidote to the cancerous racism and poverty that has affected so many lives. The black Jesus humanized young people living in conditions meant to dehumanize them.

Declaring that Jesus was an Afro-Asiatic Jew is a call to reconciliation and unity. Just the phrase "Afro-Asiatic Jew" implies an image of a Jesus who crossed boundaries and created relationships. My preaching experiences in South Africa have been as diverse as the cities and their people. I have preached in a white Afrikaans-speaking Dutch Reformed Church. I have also preached at a township congregation where the leader asked that I be given a Zulu welcome in Zulu time as the worship team broke into Zulu hymns and the congregation danced in the aisles—a day later I spoke at a church in the Phoenix Township of Durban where half a million Indians reside.

Declaring that Jesus was an Afro-Asiatic Jew offers an opportunity for repentance, forgiveness, and true reconciliation. On one visit to South Africa, I spoke with several young pastors from the Dutch Reformed Church. They shared with me how they had rejected the apartheid theology in which they were raised. Many wanted their congregations to be multiracial and multicultural. The progressive pastors I met were struggling sincerely with how to repair the damage of the past and move forward into an unknown future. I listened closely to their challenges and apprehensions. I sensed in some a very deep cry to rediscover their own sense of humanity after having lived under the dictates of a theology that provided support for the inhumane crimes committed by the apartheid government. Whites in South Africa, and in the United States, must embrace a homecoming journey as a part of their healing and for their own inclusion in a nation where persons of color are engaging on such a path.

I preached at a Dutch Reformed congregation that had voted to be multicultural. The Sunday service included the confirmation liturgy—all in Afrikaans. The congregation was still predominately white, so all of the young people being confirmed were white. The parents of these youth had participated in the same tradition when they were younger. But these young people experienced something that their parents, when they were youth, never would have thought possible or even desirable. Two pastors from the congregation, one white and one black, officiated at the communion portion of the confirmation liturgy. It was a small change but symbolically significant for these young people and their future as persons called to live in a fellowship that seeks to be a community for all of God's children.

The Jesus Was Black Tour also availed me the opportunity to preach to a multicultural crowd at the Cathedral Church of St. George in Cape Town. The Mass at this high-church Anglican congregation included incense and the ringing of bells. It is also home to the archbishop; Desmond Tutu presided during his tenure as archbishop. Father Terrance Lester, the canon missioner and presiding priest for the Mass, greeted me when I arrived. He asked if I wanted to be fully vested. I was not completely sure what that meant, but I agreed. I was escorted into a room and Fr. Lester proceeded to clothe me with the robe and vestments of an Anglican priest. Then he tied around my waist a rope, called the girdle, that hangs down. As he put it on me, Fr. Lester stated, "This is Father Desmond's girdle." What an honor and thrill! Here I was a "white" man from the United States wearing the girdle of a South African archbishop of reconciliation while declaring to an enthusiastic congregation the message of an Afro-Asiatic Jesus.

❄❄❄

In his book *Jesus and the Disinherited*, Howard Thurman asked, "What [do] the teachings and the life of Jesus have to say to those who stand, at a moment in human history, with their backs against the wall. . . . The masses of [people] live with their backs constantly against the wall. They are the poor, the disinherited, the dispossessed. What does our religion say to them?"[1] Thurman challenged the assumption that Christianity is limited to telling Christian people to help the poor. Rather, it is, as Bishop Ruiz said at the Salzburg Seminar, a religion *of* the poor.

So often we want to do the work of religion rather than be healed and transformed by our faith in God. All of us experience some form of poverty? How does our religious faith speak to our impoverished core identity and create healing homecoming moments? The black Jesus I spoke of in South Africa did that in deeply profound ways. In subsequent visits to South Africa, persons who heard these messages have recounted how they rediscovered a lost part of their sense of humanity. Persons of color testified to the transformation that had occurred in their own lives. Their "blackness" was redeemed. They could now fully embrace the fact that they *were* created in the image of God. I have observed humanity restored in the lives of individuals of all races who had internalized the dehumanizing perspective of the oppressor. The "whiteness" of the image of Jesus was used historically to support the notion that whites were superior and persons of color were inferior. Dismantling this lie allowed whites and persons of color to reject a racialized definition of who is created in the image of God. This produced a homecoming with their humanity.

During the Jesus Was Black Tour, a black student at the Biblical Institute—Eastern Cape in Port Elizabeth gave me a powerful gift. At the end of my lecture he stood to express gratitude on behalf of the class for my remarks. He spoke about how he had hated whites for so long, especially Boers (Afrikaners). As he spoke I thought of my common Dutch heritage with the Afrikaners. He thanked God for the change in his life and how he appreciated my commitment to reconciliation. As a gift from the class, he read from the Scriptures. This action and the words of Scripture he declared spoke well of how his humanity had been restored by God through the reconciliation process occurring in South Africa.

Now who will harm you if you are eager to do what is good? But even if you do suffer for doing what is right, you are

blessed. Do not fear what they fear, and do not be intimidated, but in your hearts sanctify Christ as Lord. Always be
ready to make your defense to anyone who demands from
you an accounting for the hope that is in you; yet do it with
gentleness and reverence. Keep your conscience clear, so
that, when you are maligned, those who abuse you for your
good conduct in Christ may be put to shame. For it is better
to suffer for doing good, if suffering should be God's will,
than to suffer for doing evil (1 Peter 3:13-17).

Dismantling white supremacy is hard and difficult work—
especially in the context of our religious faith, where our
deepest values reside. I have learned to expect tensions and
discomfort. Change usually does not happen instantaneously.
It is a process. I have become content with the fact that much
of what I do plants seeds of truth that might set us free, restore
our sense of being created in the image of God, and produce
a homecoming with our humanity as children of God. As
Jesus stated, "The truth will make you free" (John 8:32).

✳✳✳

Archbishop Desmond Tutu embodies the inclusive spirit of an
Afro-Asiatic Jesus. On our final day in South Africa in 2002, we
spent forty minutes as a family visiting with Archbishop Tutu at
his office in Cape Town, an incredible honor and delight. He
was in good health and continuing to work for reconciliation
in South Africa, as well as in places like Israel-Palestine. Our
Cape Town hosts, Njabulo and Mpho Ndebele, were friends
of the Tutu family since childhood. They were kind enough to
arrange our visit.

As someone who has committed his life to reconciliation,
I felt particularly fortunate to be sitting with the Nobel Prize
laureate. This was a highly valued moment for me. I immediately
asked Archbishop Tutu a question related to reconciliation. He

kindly offered a serious answer to my query. Then he paused and turned to my twelve-year-old son, Jonathan, and asked him about his interests. When Jonathan finished speaking, I instantly asked another question. I knew this was a rare occasion. Tutu answered and then spoke to my fifteen-year-old daughter, Rachel, asking about her interests. When Rachel was finished, I was again overcome by the feeling that this was a once-in-a-lifetime opportunity to dialogue with one of history's most noted reconcilers. I asked yet another question. The archbishop took time to respond, and then he looked toward my wife Karen and asked about her work.

This scenario demonstrates how inclusive Desmond Tutu is in whom he values as worthy of his attention. No one was left out despite my efforts to dominate the time. Every person counts. Archbishop Tutu was not enamored with himself. He has discovered his humanity and does not allow others to treat him as more than human or less than human. My efforts to facilitate the repair and restoration of a sense of humanity among indigenous black Africans, whites, Indians, and Coloureds in South Africa have been divine opportunities. But my visits to South Africa are occasional gestures and small contributions. Archbishop Desmond Tutu and many others have fought daily against dehumanization and struggled for the recognition that we all bear the divine image. Such efforts are at the center of what is necessary for all of us to experience being at home in our humanity. We left the archbishop's office that day farther down the road to our redemption and closer to the realization of homecoming. We had been in the presence of an individual so very at home with his essence as a child of God. And his comfort with his own personhood made us feel more at home.

CHAPTER SEVEN

The Peace of Jerusalem

I left for Tel Aviv, Israel, after a thorough interrogation at the Schiphol Airport in Amsterdam. My stay in Egypt prior to heading for Israel seemed to trigger security concerns. The flight arrived at the Ben Gurion International Airport in the middle of a January night in 2006. I cleared customs and left the airport at two o'clock in the morning, riding in a taxi cab on the highway to East Jerusalem where I was staying. Before long the flashing police lights of a flying checkpoint demanded that my Palestinian taxi driver stop his car. The Israeli police officer spoke to the driver and then directed a huge high beam flashlight through the window into the back seat, where I fumbled for my passport to identify myself as a citizen of the United States. This was my welcome to the Holy Land.

At 8:00 a.m., I was awakened by the alarm clock at my residence on the Mount of Olives. I stepped outside to enjoy the wonderful view of Jerusalem and reflected on the biblical story of Jesus' triumphal entry into the Holy City from this very location. My first few hours in the Holy Land clearly illustrated the reality of Palestine and Israel, a mixed experience: ancient and modern, religious and secular, exciting and stressful, spiritual and painful. It was thrilling to visit the holy sites and to be in places that I had heard about all my life—to walk where Jesus walked. At the same time, every day I experienced the deep throbbing pain of this land. I soon discovered that in modern Jerusalem one rarely experiences the city of peace.

After a few hours of sleep on the morning of my arrival, World Vision staff took me to some small Palestinian villages near Bethlehem. They wanted me immediately to experience life in the Occupied Palestinian Territories. A few minutes after leaving the Mount of Olives, I was confronted by the Wall. Israel considers it a security wall. Many Palestinians call it the apartheid wall. Building a wall to divide Israel and Palestine distressed and discouraged me, and it offended my sensibilities given my reconciliation instincts. This wall effectively claimed for Israel valuable portions of land granted to the Palestinians in the 1948 accord and occupied by Israel since 1967. The wall isolated Palestinian villages from access to much needed resources. I was informed that Palestinian villages and neighborhoods that were in the path of the wall were being destroyed. I saw where people's homes had been demolished with little warning. I observed olive trees that were uprooted, causing Palestinians to lose an important source of income. The wall also served as a psychological barrier—it felt dehumanizing. Both Palestinian and Israeli Jewish human rights organizations challenged this process of wall building.

In a small town near Bethlehem, I met village council members and residents. Twenty-six homes had been demolished by the Israeli government. I was told that invoices for the cost of the demolition were sent to each of the Palestinian homeowners, now without homes, rather than to the State of Israel. We met one man who had secured a court order to stop the destruction of his home just as they began tearing down the side of his house. Five families lived in his home—a total of twenty-one people. He lived with the unsettling awareness that his house could still be demolished the next day. We were told of another man who "lost his mind" when he found his home turned into rubble. As Palestinian homes and villages were demolished, new Jewish settlements in the West Bank were being built. A political agenda fueled this process of destruction and building.

Palestine was a stressful place filled with the daily indignities of check points and unequal resources determined by neighborhood identity (despite equal taxation). Israel controlled the water in Palestinian lands and sold it back to the Palestinians. I was told how some Jewish settlements in the West Bank dumped their sewage into Palestinian areas. There was an Israeli military presence everywhere. I began to understand more fully why people participated in uprisings. One feels frustrated, angry, and without options. What do you have to lose? My many visits to South Africa equipped me with a lens that saw apartheid like conditions in the Occupied Palestinian Territories. I thought the Palestinian situation must be much like living in apartheid South Africa.

On that first day in the village I heard a buzzing sound overhead. When I asked what was making the sound, someone informed me that it was an Israeli surveillance drone. I was unnerved by this occurrence. So this was occupation. The village seemed so quiet and peaceful. Why were they under surveillance? Now somewhat paranoid, I even wondered irrationally if I was being watched. I could barely keep from crying much of the afternoon. I struggled to keep my composure and not explode with rage. This was after only one day in Palestine and Israel. What must it feel like to live here day after day?

The situation felt so immoral, and it was happening in the streets, neighborhoods, and villages where Jesus preached, healed, and walked. Most Christians in the Holy Land are Palestinians. I reflected on the reality that followers of Jesus in the twenty-first century were under occupation and experienced persecution much like Jesus' fellow Jews did in the first century under the occupation of the Roman Empire.

I was so emotionally exhausted from my first day in Palestine that I was glad for day two, which would focus on visiting the holy sites. Perhaps there I could find some peace in Jerusalem. I visited the Dome of the Rock (one of Islam's holiest sites), the Western "Wailing" Wall (Judaism's holiest site), and the Church of the Holy Sepulchre (built on the traditional sites of the empty tomb of Jesus and Golgotha—the place of Jesus' crucifixion). The old city of Jerusalem is a very small area, and these holiest places for three religious traditions are located very close together. The Temple Mount is the place where Solomon built his temple, and later Herod rebuilt the temple in the same place. Herod's temple was destroyed in A.D. 70, and all that remained was a portion of the wall—the Western or Wailing Wall. The Dome of the Rock is built on top of the Temple Mount, or the *Harem-esh-Sharif* (Noble Sanctuary), as Muslims call the place, and marks where Muhammad temporarily ascended into heaven. The Dome of the Rock was built not long after Muhammad died, making Jerusalem the third holiest city in Islam (after Mecca and Medina).

These two revered sites inhabit basically the same place. I first went through the Muslim security check to visit the magnificently beautiful Dome of the Rock. I was allowed on the grounds but not into the Dome or the Al Asqa mosque at the site. These sanctuaries were closed to non-Muslims after Ariel Sharon toured the Temple Mount in 2000. The late Yasser Arafat considered Sharon's visit offensive and ordered that only Muslims could enter these sanctuaries. After I left the grounds of the Dome of the Rock, I went through an Israeli security check to enter the space where Jews pray at the Western Wall. As I drew close to the "Wailing" Wall, I was moved by the fervor and passion of the prayers of those gathered both in the section for men and the area for women. I obtained a paper skullcap available for individuals who had not come prepared to pray and joined the men at the wall. I touched the wall, prayed, and then left. One learns in Jerusalem that sharing space does not automatically translate into peace and reconciliation.

After visiting these holy sites of Judaism and Islam, I ventured a few blocks to the Church of the Holy Sepulchre. The church was built in the fourth century on the place where tradition says that Jesus was crucified at Golgotha and buried in a nearby tomb. I entered the church and was escorted through the building by a guide I met at the door. Many Christians at the church were on a pilgrimage to Jerusalem. One group arrived singing as they entered the church. The Church of the Holy Sepulchre attracts people from all nations and church communions to a common space for prayer. Christians are often profoundly affected by their visit to this place that holds such meaning to the Jesus story—crucifixion and resurrection. The Church of the Holy Sepulchre has a symbolic centrality unlike any other church. As at other holy places, I sought to understand the reverence given to this place. I touched the place where the tomb is enclosed, as well as the rock of Golgotha.

I learned while walking through the Church of the Holy Sepulchre that six different churches each controlled a section of the building—Greeks, Armenians, Copts, Ethiopians, Syrians, and Roman Catholics. Throughout history these church communions have fought each other for control of this most holy site, sometimes violently. This often has occurred at the prompting of the nation states with vested interests in the symbolic power of this church, even up to the present. Over eight hundred years ago, the Muslim Sultan Saladin entrusted the key for the only door at the church to a Muslim man from the Nuseibeh family. Every morning he would open the door to the church. Every evening he would close and lock the door. This greatly reduced tensions among the Christian church communions. His family has continued this task ever since. At the end of my walk through the church, my tour guide handed me his business card and introduced himself as Wajeeh Nuseibeh, the latest member of the family to be the door keeper. I remarked to him that it takes a Muslim to keep peace among the churches. Sadly, I did not find the peace of Jerusalem at the holy sites.

I had the amazing opportunity to be in the Holy Land during the Palestinian elections of January 2006, which occurred on my third day in Jerusalem. There was a heavy Israeli military presence due to threats of violence. Unexpectedly, I felt a greater sense of peace on this day than on previous days. The voting was very orderly and nonviolent. Of course, the world was shocked to learn of the Hamas victory (I think Hamas was equally surprised). The Palestinian people had tired of the corruption in their government and the lack of movement in the peace process, so they voted for change.

Visiting Palestine at this historic time of elections enriched my understanding. In conversations with Palestinian activists, I learned that we in the West had a one-dimensional view of Hamas. Yes, they had members that respond to Israeli occupation with horrific and unconscionable violence that must be condemned. But Hamas was not a monolithic organization. There were moderate voices. Hamas had very significant social service initiatives in some of the poorest areas. Many hoped that the entrance of Hamas into the election process suggested a change in their approach. All sides need to renounce violence and sit down at the table of reconciliation dialogue. Unfortunately, Israel, the United States, the United Nations, and much of the world (including some Arab countries) did not give Hamas any opportunity to show a different face. In a surreal moment, a few days later we turned onto a street in Bethlehem and found ourselves in the midst of an impromptu Hamas victory parade of twenty or so cars with young men waving the Hamas flag.

On the day of the elections, most Palestinians were off work to stand in line to vote. So I spent the day in West Jerusalem meeting with Israeli human rights organizations and Jewish peace and reconciliation activists. It was very significant for me to see the passion and commitment of Israeli Jews who hungered for justice and peace in Jerusalem. Their willingness to hold the Israeli government accountable for human rights and the social justice demands of Judaism was encouraging.

As a person committed to social justice and the ministry of reconciliation, the purpose of my trip was to understand better the conditions causing the hostilities in Palestine and Israel. I spoke with Israeli human rights activists, Palestinian grassroots community development leaders, religious leaders, and people in villages and neighborhoods. What I saw and experienced was deeply disturbing and troubling. One cannot escape the presence of the Israeli military and police. Everywhere I saw teenage soldiers (both men and women) carrying very large automatic weapons. Security checkpoints were common at the borders between Israel and the Occupied Palestinian Territories. Palestinians often waited long hours to get through. Sometimes they were strip searched. Sometimes they were refused entry. "Flying" checkpoints appeared randomly.

I find it difficult to describe the feeling of life in such a pressurized setting. The daily indignities were stressful on families and individuals. They undermine the dignity and hopes of people. Sometimes they were big things like walls and racial profiling. Other times they seemed small, like stoplights at intersections that allow two to four minutes for vehicles traveling to and from Israel to cross and seven to nine seconds at the same intersection for cars crossing from Palestinian areas. Due to the occupation I would think that every Palestinian was on the verge of exploding emotionally, if not violently. This reality created an intense fear among Israelis, who also live under the daily stress of this environment.

During my stay, I searched for the peace of Jerusalem. I wanted to experience God in the Holy City. This was difficult to accomplish with all of the tourist trappings of the holy sites and the intense stress of the occupation. The Spirit of God did break through the noise and confusion, however, with the melodies of Jerusalem. One day in the Old City of Jerusalem, I was eating lunch on the rooftop of a restaurant. At 11:45 in the morning, a Muslim cleric sounded the call to prayer from the Dome of the Rock. After ten minutes or so, he grew quiet. Then at noon the bells of the Lutheran Church of the Redeemer rang out. Oh, the melodies of Jerusalem.

On my last day in Jerusalem in 2006, I walked down the side of the Mount of Olives with the glorious view of the Old City. I came to the Church of All Nations in the Garden of Gethsemane and entered seeking some solace during my final hours in Jerusalem. In the quiet of the sanctuary sat a women whose body was rocking back and forth as she prayed silently to herself. Soon she began to sing. Her beautifully angelic voice filled the acoustically rich sanctuary with little effort. I did not understand her language. Then I heard her Middle Eastern–flavored voice sing repeatedly, "Hallelujah!" This universal word of praise and worship reminded me that God is still very much present in the city of Jerusalem—and this was the true melody of the city of peace.

✳✳✳

I returned to Jerusalem for a second visit one year later, in January of 2007. The purpose of my second visit was to deepen both my understanding of the conflict and my relationships with the peacemakers. In particular I sought more interaction with Jews and Muslims working for peace. I had the opportunity to visit new places, including Nazareth, Hebron, Tel Aviv, Ramallah, and Netanya, as well as to stand at the Sea of Galilee and the Mediterranean Sea. I visited the very powerful Yad Vashem (Holocaust museum) in Jerusalem. I was moved by the visit and very troubled by the anti-Semitism of the Nazis and the ways our world still struggles with this bigotry and other prejudices.

We must never forget the tragedy and trauma of the Holocaust, which still casts a large shadow over all that happens in Israel.

I went to Bethlehem to see Zougbhi Zougbhi again, a member of the city council and the director of Wi'am—the Palestinian Conflict Resolution Centre. I stayed overnight at the home of Zoughbi's brother Nicola and wife Laurette. In the morning, Laurette prepared the most amazing breakfast: pickled egg plant, pickled cauliflower, stuffed cabbage rolls, and a wonderful assortment of sauces in which to dip pieces of pita bread (homemade plum jelly, yogurt sauce, raisin juice and honey sauce, and more). I ate like a Palestinian while staying with the Zougbhis. I visited Galilee for the first time and breathed deeply the same air that Jesus inhaled while walking the streets of Nazareth. On this second visit to the Holy Land, I met peacemakers who witnessed to what is possible. They were Christian, Muslim, and Jewish.

In the village of Ibillin, Galilee, in Israel, I met Archbishop Elias Chacour of the Melkite Catholic Church (the largest communion of Christians in the Holy Land). I had read his book *Blood Brothers*, so I knew of his ministry of reconciliation.[1] As a Palestinian Christian he reaches out with great love to his Jewish and Muslim brothers and sisters. His love for Israeli Jews is quite amazing given that his own family was forcibly removed from their home during the 1948 Nakba ("catastrophe") at the formation of the modern State of Israel. Archbishop Chacour spoke of how the churches of Palestinian Christians date back to the first century. Palestinian Christians were the remnant of Jesus' followers from the first century church in Palestine noted in the biblical story when the author of Acts stated that Arabs were present on the Day of Pentecost (Acts 2:11). Chacour noted that Palestinian Christians therefore feel a deep and intimate connection to Jesus and the first-century church. "For God a thousand years is like a day . . . so Jesus hung out with us and our families two days ago." I was overwhelmed by the love expressed by Palestinian Christians like Chacour toward Jewish people, whom they see as their brothers and sisters in the Holy Land. Many express a desire to share the land in peace, to live together. As Archbishop Chacour stated, "You are welcome with us, but not without us."

Archbishop Chacour proclaimed reconciliation from Galilee, the largest concentration of Palestinian Arabs within the State of Israel. I also found peacemakers in the West Bank. One afternoon I visited the small Palestinian village of Bi'lin near Ramallah in the West Bank of the Occupied Palestinian Territories. The Israeli government built the separation-apartheid wall right through the middle of this town, separating the olive groves and gardens from the residential areas. This makes it very difficult for Palestinians to earn a living. A group of Bi'lin citizens formed a nonviolent direct action group to address this injustice. Every Friday, after noon prayers in the Mosque, they would protest against the construction of the wall. The Palestinian Gandhis, as they were called, were always joined by Israeli Jewish peace activists and international protesters. They were regularly tear-gassed and sometimes arrested by the soldiers at the check point. The protest movement in Bi'lin was a classic civil rights struggle, taking action both in the courts and on the streets.

I was inspired by the stories told by Abedallah Abu-Rahma, a leader of the Bi'lin movement. After the conversation, Abedallah took me to the site of their protests. The wall in the more rural areas is actually a high fence with barbed wire. As we got closer to the Israeli checkpoint, Abedallah began to hit the fence. This was not allowed, but he continued to bang the fence with his fist as a statement of his humanity. This triggered a surveillance camera on a high tower, which turned and captured us in full view. The soldiers demanded that Abedallah stop. But he continued his act of defiance. There was quite an argument at the checkpoint about who could pass. Finally, this was resolved and Bi'lin residents crossed. Abedallah led us to where the weekly protests take place. Here he stooped down, grasped something, and presented it to me. It was a spent tear gas canister from the previous protest. Abedallah said that this would remind me of my visit to Bi'lin and their struggle for human rights and liberation.

I also discovered Israeli Jews who were busy with the work of peace, as well as people working together across the lines of religion. I spent a day at a conference in Netanya, Israel, called "Third Party Involvement in the Peace Process." The Vice Prime Minister of Israel, Shimon Peres, was the keynote speaker, along with ambassadors, United Nations staff, and human rights activists. It was an Israeli conference attended by government leaders and NGO directors. The conference was a bit stuffy, basically a bunch of people dressed in professional business attire. But I had the opportunity to accompany the leading actors in the unexpected drama of the day—the Jerusalem Peacemakers: Eliyahu McLean (an observant Israeli Jewish interfaith reconciliation leader), Sheikh Abdul Aziz Bukhari (a Sufi Muslim reconciliation leader), and Ibrahim Ahmad Abu El-Hawa (a Muslim peacemaker). They were dressed in regalia representing their various traditions: Eliyahu as an orthodox Jew, the Sheikh in his religious garb, and Ibrahim in traditional Arab attire.

We arrived late, and the conference was in full swing. As Shimon Peres was giving his keynote address, into the room burst this colorful threesome. All eyes turned in the direction of these three Jerusalem Peacemakers. Throughout the rest of the day, they were the center of attention. What I saw in action was the enactment of a public parable of peace. Eliyahu, Ibrahim, and Sheikh Bukhari visually communicated the possibility that friendship can exist across the lines of religion and culture. They also spoke clearly to each person who came to meet them, in this very secular gathering, that people of faith must be included in the peace process if reconciliation is the desired outcome.

A few days later I joined Eliyahu and Sheikh Bukhari to visit the Orthodox Jewish outpost settlement of Tekoa in the West Bank, which is the ancestral home of the biblical prophet Amos. Palestinians are deeply affronted by the construction of these settlements and consider them not only illegal but an insult to their dignity. The Orthodox Jews who construct and dwell in outposts like Tekoa believe that God gave them this land and that they are simply living on land promised to them. The tensions between Israeli Jews in Tekoa and neighboring Palestinian Arabs in the much older village of Teqoa (Tuqu') are unstable and explosive.

Upon arrival in Tekoa, Eliyahu and I left Sheikh Bukhari at the car and proceeded to bask in the panorama of a picturesque canyon located at Tekoa called by local Palestinians Wadi Khareitoun (Khreiton), or the Chariton Valley, after Saint Chariton, a founder of monastic life in the Judean Desert. As we gazed across this parched desert canyon, we could envisage Amos standing where we stood, mesmerized by visions and prophetic words conveyed by the Almighty. The canyon had a mystical quality to it. I felt like I could reach out and almost touch the divine. The canyon visit left me with a deep sense of awe that I cannot articulate in words. When we returned from our brief excursion to enjoy the mystery of the canyon, the car was surrounded by four gun-toting young men from the town. The Sheikh said that they had been interrogating him. It seems they were not happy to have an Arab in their town. Eliyahu informed the young vigilantes with automatic weapons that we were in town to visit Rabbi Menachem Froman, a highly revered and respected rabbi in Tekoa nationally known for his peacemaking efforts and also a member of the Jerusalem Peacemakers. This seemed to ease the tensions a bit, but the young men remained upset that we had not informed them that we would be in their town. The transcendent peaceful calm of the majestic canyon was quickly interrupted by this ugly act of violent bravado.

Shortly thereafter we were stopped by a police officer (sort of a Rambo type character). Most likely the four young men we had encountered earlier reported our presence in their town. The burly police officer questioned us about why were in town and asked to see identification. He said he did not need to see the identification of Eliyahu (the Jew). He did not even open my United States passport. But he looked quite thoroughly at the ID presented by the Arab Sheikh. The officer said that Eliyahu and I were not a problem. He then pointed at Sheikh Bukhari and said he was a problem. The officer asked me if I knew why he was a problem. I said I did not. Then he switched to Hebrew and spoke at some length about why Arabs were a problem for Israel.

When the police officer paused for a moment, Eliyahu shared with him that we were on a mission of peace among people of different religions. We were traveling together as a Jew, a Muslim, and a Christian. Surprisingly, this caused the officer's attitude to soften a bit. He recounted that he had migrated to Israel from Chile where people of many religions lived side-by-side. At this point both Eliyahu and Sheikh Bukhari greeted the police officer with, "Hola! Cómo estás." The officer began to laugh and a situation full of tension and stereotypes was humanized into a friendly interchange. He then released us to continue our travels.

We finally found Rabbi Froman at his home, where we enjoyed some wonderful moments with him and his family. It was a true honor and blessing to be in the presence of this wise and kind rabbi. Rabbi Froman is an unusual orthodox settler rabbi. He was one of the founders of the Zionist settler movement. He lives in a Jewish settlement—an outpost in the Palestinian territories. But he is also an activist for peace inspired by the Scriptures and his love for God. This has given him close relationships with many Palestinians, both Muslims and Christians. His passion for peace led him to form friendships with the late Yassar Arafat and the late Sheikh Ahmed Yassin, the spiritual founder of Hamas (who was assassinated by an Israeli helicopter missile strike on his car as he left a mosque in Gaza). Although the rabbi feels called to live in Tekoa, he does not feel allied with the Israeli government. He has stated that he is willing to live under the State of Israel or a new Palestinian state, whether governed by Fatah or Hamas.

With his long white beard Rabbi Froman looks like a modern day Amos in Tekoa. When we arrived he was preparing to lead evening prayers. As he repeatedly hugged Sufi Muslim Sheikh Bukhari, he noted affectionately that when he lost track of time, the Muslim call to prayer would always remind him that it was time for him to pray also. I gave Rabbi Froman a copy of my book *Reconciliation*. As he looked at the book, he told an old story from the rabbis. It seems that someone asked God what the divine had been doing since finishing work on the sixth day of creation. God replied that the Almighty's post-creation work was matching people, in other words, reconciliation. Rabbi Froman added that as followers of God, our work should also be reconciliation. Furthermore, according to the rabbi, reconciliation was our greatest act of worship.

✳✳✳

I have been deeply affected by my visits to Jerusalem and the Holy Land. The first few nights that I was home, after my first visit, my dreams were filled with the stress of check points and the occupation in Palestine. For at least a week, I struggled in my dreams with my inability to speak Arabic. For more than two weeks my dreams transported me to Palestine. My dreams simply confirmed the imprint on my soul that occurred as a result of my time in Jerusalem and the West Bank. I felt a psychic and spiritual link to Palestine. I sensed that I would have an ongoing relationship with Palestine and Israel in the future as it relates to reconciliation. I have no idea what this means. Certainly such a relationship will influence my understanding of reconciliation and how I teach and inspire others in this work. Perhaps there will even be a small role for me to play at some point in the future. It is all in God's hands. The land of Palestine-Israel is a wonderful and challenging place. Although it is a small place, it is at the center of the world's attention. Jerusalem is at the epicenter of world events. When Jerusalem finds peace it will affect the entire globe.

As I reflected on my time in Palestine and Israel, as well as the lingering effects after my return, I recognized what might be another divine expectation for the next phase of my life. In New York City, I felt called to work for reconciliation and social justice regarding urban and multicultural challenges in the United States. This calling still continues. In Salzburg, I sensed an invitation to engage with global realities, which was realized in Johannesburg and elsewhere in South Africa. This calling still continues. Jerusalem released a second impulse embedded in the Salzburg experience. I was empowered to embrace the work of peace, social justice, and reconciliation in multi-religious and interfaith settings. I await the outcome of this divine expectation.

Roots in Africa

In 1678 a small ship from Madagascar arrived in the British colony of Massachusetts in North America. The ocean voyage from the eastern coastal side of the continent of Africa to North America took twenty months. This ship brought forty to fifty black Africans, mostly women and children, to sell to citizens of colonial Massachusetts. The slave trade along the east coast of Africa and the island of Madagascar was a lucrative business for Arab and European exporters. In the 1670s, English and American colonists were engaged in trade directly with the East African ports, as well as stealing from Arab and European ships. I wonder if the parents of my ancestor Thomas Bedoona were among the forty to fifty Africans on that vessel arriving in Massachusetts in 1678. Perhaps Thomas himself was one of the children on board the ship, having been born before or during the voyage with his birth date being established as the same as his arrival date. If his parents were on that ship, it is more likely that he was born after the ship arrived as most genealogists have it in 1680.[1]

Africans arriving in the Americas did not have English names and seldom retained their own names. Sometimes they were given an English first name and the slave master's last name. Other times they just had a first name with "the Negro" after it. Obviously, Thomas was an English name given to him, probably at birth in Roxbury. Thomas's surname Bedoona is certainly not an English name. Perhaps his surname is a clue to Thomas Bedoona's origins. At the time that my mother announced this significant ancestral discovery, I was auditing an Introduction to Arabic course. The surname Bedoona sounded much like the Arabic words and phrases I was learning. One scholar I spoke with thought that perhaps the name derived from the Arabic word *bedouin*. This would imply that Thomas or his parents came from an Arabic-speaking part of Africa and took this name to describe a life that had become nomadic. This book has described my nomadic journey of homecoming with my humanity. In many ways, my journey has been that of a *bedouin*. My cultural identity has wandered the human landscape and established multiple places that resonate with a sense of home.

The Arabic word *bedoon* means "without." It is used in some Arabic-speaking countries to refer to groups of people who do not have a national identity or ethnic home. This is certainly true for what I know of Thomas Bedoona today. He is a person mentioned in history without a national home, parents, or identity. Thomas Bedoona and his parents may have felt that in the Americas they had lost any sense of belonging or home. They were experiencing life without a place to call home. A sense of homelessness describes the identity many of us hold. African Americans still struggle with the loss of cultural, national, and religious identity that occurred through slavery. Malcolm X and members of the Nation of Islam replaced their European last names with an X to signify the loss of their names. Thomas Bedoona reminds us that many feel like they are *bedoon*, without a home, an identity, or a feeling of being fully human.

Just because I cannot find any reference to Thomas Bedoona's national identity does not mean that he was without one or was unaware of his origins. I searched the internet using the various spellings of Bedoona, hoping to solve this mystery. When I used the alternate spelling "Bedouna," I was directed to the work of Abu Abd Allah Muhammad al-Idrisi al-Qurtubi al-Hasani (al-Idrisi), the noted Arab geographer and explorer of the twelfth century. A city called Bedouna, or sometimes Baduna, is found in al-Idrisi's writings and on his maps at the Horn of Africa. Bedouna has been variously identified as Barawa or Mogadishu in present day Somalia. In the fourteenth century, Europeans Marino Sanudo and Pietro Vesconte, in a book about the Crusades, noted an area in the same region they called Bedona. Perhaps for Thomas and his parents, using the surname Bedoona was a way of holding onto their home, their place of origin. Maybe it was more like Thomas from the city of Bedouna. This was often a way of identifying oneself, like Saul of Tarsus or Jesus of Nazareth in the biblical narratives.[2]

If Thomas' parents were from Bedouna, then my ancestor was quite likely from an African Muslim family. Now that is an interesting symbolic link given that the global portion of my journey has so often been in Africa and navigating contexts where Islam is strong. My journey from Johannesburg to Jerusalem has taken me through the intersection of global cultures and religious faiths. On this homecoming journey, I discovered a much larger cultural and religious world than I could have imagined while interacting with people from forty nations at a conference in Salzburg, enjoying a healing moment of full humanity in South Africa, and experiencing a taste of peace in Jerusalem.

Traveling from Harlem to Roxbury and from Johannesburg to Jerusalem radically altered and joyously affirmed the essence of my identity. I am a child of God. I am a white male of Dutch and English ancestry with one drop of African blood who is a citizen of the United States. My cultural self-understanding has been affected by socialization in African American communities and the consciousness raised by multiple visits to South

Africa and Palestine-Israel. As a person with race, class, and male privilege, I have committed my life to social justice and reconciliation. The collision of birthright privilege and experiential transformation invites me everyday to embrace a homecoming with my humanity, created in the image of God.

Epilogue

The Homecoming Dance

I began this book by sharing about my "tears at a homecoming" in South Africa when I first visited in 2000. When I returned to South Africa with my family in 2002 to speak at the same conference, I was apprehensive about what would happen on this visit, because the experience had been so deeply felt and intensely profound in 2000. Whenever I tried to tell people about that sacred moment of homecoming with God, I would experience again the emotions, and tears would begin to well up in my eyes. When I arrived at the conference center in Lenasia, South Africa, I spoke with two leaders who had attended the conference in 2000. They asked if I was going to cry again this time. I appreciated and enjoyed their humor, which is an expression of familial affection for many in South Africa. But when I began to speak to them of that primal moment of homecoming with my humanity, the emotions started to flood my spirit again.

The conference began on a Wednesday evening. I decided that on the first night I would speak of the tears I shed in 2000, since many in attendance had witnessed the prior event. As part of the introductory remarks before my message, I spoke of that "homecoming" event on my previous visit and the tears it produced. Of course, my emotions refused to stay in check. I told the crowd that I made no promises that I would not cry again. "I feel things very deeply," I acknowledged. Then

I preached my sermon. On Friday evening in my opening
remarks before the sermon, I referred back to the comments
I had made on Wednesday night. I told the assembled crowd
that I felt my open and transparent sharing had produced
an intimacy between us that allowed for me to reveal more
of my struggles. I stated that I needed to confess something.
Furthermore, this issue had become so troublesome that it
was affecting my marriage. At this point I peered out at the
audience and noticed that several individuals were appearing
quite squeamish and very uncomfortable. Some were so vis-
ibly disturbed by the direction that my remarks were headed
that I thought they might quickly get up and leave. The last
thing that congregants want to hear is a confession of sin from
a preacher.

So I continued, "I must confess that I cannot dance."
Laughter broke out, and there was a great sense of relief for
many that I was *not* confessing some horrible sexual sin. I told
the group that I had been raised in a home that did not dance.
Therefore, I missed that critical point in a child's life when
rhythm is nurtured. To make matters worse, my wife loves to
dance and her husband is untalented in this area. I then said
that if anyone at the conference had the gift of dance and
felt the Spirit telling them to help me in this area, I welcomed
the opportunity for instruction. Then I preached my sermon.
The conference did not have a preaching service on Saturday
evening. We did have a beautiful sunrise service and an evening concert instead. In the early evening on that Saturday,
I walked by Joy Nxumalo, a youth minister from Swaziland,
instructing a group in Swazi step dance. She immediately
beckoned me to join her step dance students. Joy patiently
gave me some lessons and affirmed me in my efforts—all to
the amazement of my wife and children. Later that night a
dance choreographer in attendance also took me aside and
tried to teach me some dance moves.

At the Sunday morning service, the final event of the conference, I stepped up to the pulpit and offered my gratitude to
all who had made the week so special. Then I reminded the
group that in my Thursday sermon I had said that when God
does a miracle in our lives we need to bear witness to that fact.
I had asked for help in dance on Friday, and I needed to witness to what God had done. So I stepped out from behind the
pulpit and demonstrated my newly acquired "skills" in step
dance, then added a few moves taught to me by the choreographer. The place erupted in shouts and applause. Joy told
me later that she jumped out of her seat in excitement and
began shouting and ululating. After the crowd quieted down,
I thanked my dance instructors. Then I preached my sermon.
And God visited us that morning.

My feeble attempts at dancing that Sunday morning had
great personal meaning because of the tie to my homecoming
experience two years earlier. I like to think of that morning
as my homecoming dance with God. The metaphor of the
homecoming dance is useful for grasping the inward side of
our relationship with God. We all need to dance with God on
the journey toward the acceptance of our full humanity—
embracing the divine image imprinted on each one of us. We
need that relationship where we can be fully known, transparent, vulnerable, and spiritually naked. We need a place of
complete trust, true liberty, and unconditional love. We need
some space for freedom and abandonment where the walls of
inhibition are torn down.

I have discovered that I need to dance with God when I
get tired on the journey. Weariness is common to those working for social justice and reconciliation. When my reserves are
low, I need to be spiritually recharged. This often happens
when I meet God in nature. The woods and the mountains
are places where I can sense the closeness of God. I regularly
walk through a wooded area in urban Minneapolis and feel

a freedom in my communication with God. Some years ago my family and I vacationed for a week in the Colorado Rocky Mountains. I had brought a new Bible with me, and I began reading the Gospel of Luke while viewing the mountains. That week in the mountains began a two-year spiritual love affair with the Luke-Acts narrative. The place where I easily find God is near water. Portions of this book were written while sitting next to some of Minnesota's many lakes.

The ocean is the place in nature where I find the greatest spiritual rest and refreshment. A most profound experience of God's grace occurred in 1994 when my wife Karen and I were on our first visit to the Islands of Hawaii. The awesome natural splendor of the island paradise, the hot bright sun, the cool sand, the soothing sound of the waves, revived my soul in countless inexpressible ways. The intensity of the experience increased while walking along the mysterious and lovely Waimanalo Beach on Oahu. The transcendent moment was set in a three-dimensional frame with mountains on one side and ocean on the other, blue sky above and sand below. I felt like I could reach out and almost hold hands with God. I left Hawaii completely rested. When people asked about our trip to the islands, my answer was that I felt like I had been in the womb of God. My weary soul had been embraced and caressed by the Creator through a spiritually embryonic homecoming experience.[1]

Life's journey also brings times of discouragement and feelings of distance from God. Once again I often find encouragement in the sanctuary of the Creator's natural settings. I have also discovered that sometimes God reaches out to me as if inviting me back to the dance. In early 1998, I felt discouraged with my work at TURN and began to consider a search for other job options. The organization had lost a major funding source, and I lacked vision and motivation. In the midst of these days of despair, I traveled to Evanston, Illinois, to speak about reconciliation at a national caucus of African American pastors and lay leaders from the National Association of the Church of God. I presented during the day sessions. Each evening we would all travel by bus to a local church for a service of singing and preaching. Evanston was in the midst of an ice storm accompanied by severely cold weather during those few days. I had brought an overcoat, but it was tattered and missing several buttons. I had to hold it together to maintain some semblance of warmth. Each night one or more of the senior women would politely but firmly chastise me for not dressing warmer. These "mothers" of the church were concerned that the "man of God" was not adequately cared for. Each time I would offer some lame excuse and thank them for their concern.

A few weeks after my return to Minneapolis, I received an anonymous package in the mail at my office. A beautiful new wool overcoat was enclosed in the box. The space on the package marked "sender" was left blank. The only clue regarding the source of the gift was the UPS station identifier—Bala Cynwyd, Pennsylvania. I surmised that perhaps one of the senior women sent it to me as a way of caring for the "man of God." I immediately interpreted the anonymous gift of the "miracle" coat as an expression of God's love and assurance in the midst of my feelings of discouragement. The mysterious gift renewed my hope. Within a few weeks I joined some pastors from the urban Hawthorne and Jordan neighborhoods in Minneapolis in a meeting to launch an eighteen-month effort that was TURN's most significant endeavor in reconciliation during my tenure. The "miracle" coat was God's way of inviting me back to life's dance in time for me to waltz into the next phase of ministry.

When dancing as a twosome, usually one person leads. In our dance with God, we sometimes try to lead. Of course this is not wise. In my life, God usually finds a way to encourage me to relinquish the attempt to lead. One day in 1997, I received a call from Rev. Richard Coleman, then pastor of St. Peter's African Methodist Episcopal Church in Minneapolis, Minnesota. He invited me to come to his church on the following evening for a reconciliation prayer service. He had invited a number of pastors primarily from African American congregations. Out of obligation to Pastor Coleman I decided to go. Honestly, I did not feel like going to a prayer service that night. I preferred to stay home and relax with my family. When I arrived at St. Peter's AME Church that evening, the prayer meeting had already begun in the basement of the church building. There were only nine of us. The focus was to be on the "in house" need for reconciliation and repentance among African Americans. The group was discussing this when I arrived. Soon the prayer time began. After some time passed the focus of the prayer shifted to the needs of each person in the gathered group.

After an hour or so, I offered a prayer for rest from weariness. I was feeling tired from the busyness of my work, writing, doctoral studies, preaching, and the like. When I finished praying, a man I had never met spoke some words to me. He had given "a word from the Lord" to some of the others. He began by telling me that I needed to run the race. I must be sure that I was running the right race. He finished by quoting a favorite New Testament passage of mine, "I have fought the good fight, I have finished the race, I have kept the faith" (2 Timothy 4:7).

After a brief pause he looked at me as if he had something more to say. Then he said that the word "reconciliation" kept coming to his mind. I had never met this man. He quoted the Bible again. This time he spoke of the "ministry of reconciliation" (2 Corinthians 5). Then he said that I needed to concentrate on the ministry of reconciliation. My focus should be "ministry." The truth of my situation was that my weariness resulted from my focus on the administration of an organization that worked for reconciliation rather than direct involvement in the ministry of reconciliation. I was leading the dance rather than allowing God to lead. It was an amazing and encouraging word that I desperately needed at that particular moment. I felt loved by God. My tendency is to express cynicism, to question if this man knew of my ministry. Could the reconciliation emphasis of his encouragement to me be a result of that knowledge? Perhaps a better question is if it matters. God spoke the word I needed to hear through this encounter.

One of my favorite meditations by Howard Thurman captures the essence of what was communicated to me that day regarding my priorities and focus.

There must be always remaining in every[one's] life some place for the singing of angels—some place for that which in itself is breathlessly beautiful and by an inherent prerogative, throwing all the rest of life into a new and creative relatedness—something that gathers up in itself all the freshets of experience from drab and commonplace areas of living and glows in one bright white light of penetrating beauty and meaning—then passes. The commonplace is shot through with new glory—old burdens become lighter, deep and ancient wounds lose much of their old, old hurting. A crown is placed over our heads that for the rest of our lives we are trying to grow tall enough to wear. Despite all the crassness of life, despite all the hardness of life, despite all of the harsh discords of life, life is saved by the singing of angels.[2]

I had allowed myself to become consumed and weighed down by the administration of reconciliation. The administrative tasks did not disappear. But rediscovering the *ministry* of reconciliation unclogged my ears so that I could hear "the singing of angels." I continue to learn how to embrace the mystical moments, the womb of God, the singing of angels in the midst of taking action for social justice and reconciliation.

One of the most unsettling yet empowering encounters I experienced of God taking the lead in the homecoming dance occurred on Father's Day in June 1994. I preached a sermon that day at the Third Street Church of God congregation in Washington, DC, a church pastored by my mentor Dr. Samuel Hines. As a way to honor Pastor Hines that morning, I decided to preach on his passion for reconciliation by using the text of 2 Corinthians 5. One of Dr. Hines' closest friends in the ministry of reconciliation, Tom Skinner, had died a few days earlier. Unbeknownst to me, not only was Pastor Hines grieving the death of his friend, he was struggling to remain encouraged about his own ministry of reconciliation. The fact that one of his sons in the ministry had embraced his passion for reconciliation and preached it in his pulpit lifted his spirits.

After the service ended, a person from the congregation came up to me and said, "The mantle has passed." This phrase comes from the story in the Hebrew Scriptures where the prophet Elijah passed on his calling to leadership to his protégé Elisha (2 Kings 2:1-15). Elijah was taken to heaven by God on a chariot of fire and dropped his mantle, or overcoat, in the process. Elisha picking up the mantle symbolized that the prophetic leadership of Elijah now rested on him. The message she spoke that day informed me that it was time to step out from behind the shadow of my mentor. It was an instructive moment in my journey. God was alerting me that I needed to follow closely as a new dance step in my life was being introduced.

That Sunday service on Father's Day in 1994 was the last time I saw my father in the ministry alive. Six months later, I was sitting next to Barbara Williams Skinner (Tom's widow) at the wake for Pastor Hines. In the middle of minor throat surgery, Samuel Hines had died unexpectedly while on the surgeon's table. Then those words, "the mantle has passed," took on a much more profound meaning and sounded a more urgent call.

Two years later I returned to preach at Third Street Church of God (now pastored by Cheryl Sanders). This was my first visit back to the church since the funeral of Samuel Hines. After the service I sought out the woman who had said, "The mantle has passed." I told her how meaningful the message had been at the time she delivered it, and even more so during the days following the death of Pastor Hines. She shared that periodically God would speak to her, in her spirit, a word for someone. She would be obedient to God and convey the message. That Sunday in June 1994, God had prodded her to speak those words to me. As Thurman wrote, "Life is saved by the singing of angels." She was an angel sent by God to me on that day in 1994.

I am one of many to whom the mantle of reconciliation and social justice ministry has been passed. As Thurman noted, "A crown is placed over our heads that for the rest of our lives we are trying to grow tall enough to wear." At times I have been reluctant to accept this mantle from God. It has not been an easy trek. But I believe there is something even more important than the divine expectation on my life. My dance with God is paramount. My personal journey to rediscover my full humanity and stay on the road to that ultimate homecoming with God consumes me. One day I will awake in the midst of "a great multitude that no one [can] count, from every nation, from all tribes, and peoples and languages, standing before the throne and before the Lamb" (Revelation 7:9). And as God wipes the tears from my eyes, I will declare boldly, I will exclaim excitedly, I will shout passionately, oh, I will sing from the depths of my soul with melodic tones, "I am home!"

The Journey Continues

Writing this book was a wonderful journey of reflection. Remembering and reliving these days confirmed lessons learned and introduced new insights. As I revisited places of joy, pain, and transformation, the stories I selected were ones that most represented the central focus of the book. I could have written of many other moments in my life that deeply affected me. There was the invitation from Dr. Frank Madison Reid III, senior pastor of the historic Bethel African Methodist Episcopal Church in Baltimore, Maryland, to speak on the subject of black men in the Bible at a men's conference hosted by the congregation in 1996.

Perhaps it was Frank's sense of humor to ask a white man to speak as an expert on black men in the Bible. I learned that he said in a Sunday sermon a few weeks after the conference, holding up my first book, *Coming Together: The Bible's Message in an Age of Diversity*, "A white man, who went to a black seminary, after having done his biblical and church historical studies, had to admit that the Europeans made Jesus white... Curtiss Paul DeYoung, a white European, who committed cultural suicide, says to counter the effects of the white Jesus it is important to proclaim that the Jesus of the Bible, who lived in Nazareth, is an Afro-Asiatic Jew."[1] I made subsequent visits to Bethel AME Church to preach. Over the course of a couple of years,

I had been in Baltimore enough for Mayor Kurt Schmoke to declare me an honorary citizen of Baltimore, Maryland, in 1998. This was a very affirming season of my life and for my research and teaching related to cultural hermeneutics and the Bible.

I could have penned some thoughts about several weeks in Milwaukee, Wisconsin, working with Robert Odom, the executive director of the Social Development Commission, on a project to connect congregations of all faiths to issues of poverty in the city. This project renewed my spirits and revived my soul after the discouragement I felt as a result of leaving the pastorate.[2] Or I could have noted a visit to the towns of Benton Harbor and St. Joseph in Michigan, where the reality of a visible, polarizing, and entrenched racial segregation tempered my hopeful view of reconciliation.

This book is limited to events during my first fifty years of life. My life journey did not pause as I was writing and editing. New adventures and fresh moments with God etched additional lines in the journal of my life. I spent the weekend of the Martin Luther King Jr. holiday in January of 2008 in Middletown, Ohio, with city and church leaders seeking a breakthrough in race relations. The publishing of *The Peoples' Bible* in the fall of 2008 completed a process of important learning.[3] I served as coeditor side-by-side with a Native American, African American, Latina, and Asian American. I also spent nearly three weeks of 2008 in the French-speaking areas of Geneva, Paris, the French Alps, and the Caribbean island of Guadeloupe. This provided a glimpse into other global realities. Nine full days of sun and sand on the beautiful island of Guadeloupe began to reproduce the experience of being in the womb of God. The first day of 2009 found me at a table of interfaith leaders in Minneapolis-St. Paul, sharing with a rare transparency about the war in Gaza. Perhaps another edition of *Homecoming* will be required at age sixty.

Writing this book reminded me again that my faith journey reflects a mystical side that defies definition. I am mysteriously drawn to what Marcus Borg calls the "thin places…where the veil momentarily lifts, and we behold God, experience the one in whom we live, all around us and within us."[4] The sacred settings of homecoming in my life have been found in locations of solitude and majestic beauty like Gethsemane, Tekoa, Waimanalo Beach, and Guadeloupe, as well as in the busy intersections of human interaction in Harlem, Johannesburg, Salzburg, and Paris. These divine locations have altered my life journey, reminded me that I am not alone, and refreshed my weary soul.

Over time I have come to embrace the fact that I have more of an artist's personality. I felt that more than ever when writing this book. This probably explains my internal dissonance when in positions that require management gifts. For me artistry and management are polar opposites. When I am being creative, I thrive. This core artist personality has enabled me to think and live outside my status quo in contexts of great cultural and religious diversity. In this reflective process, I discovered that I welcome and even seek such encounters. I have been changed by these relational and experiential encounters. I know and feel this internally. The way I view the world, and the way I understand myself, have become more multicultural. And the process continues. My inner world of ideas, worldview, and self understanding is *mestizo*—a cultural mix. Or to borrow a phrase from my friends in Guadeloupe, I am in a process of "creolization" as a result of my relational and intellectual embrace of the world that I have encountered on my homecoming journey. Without casting aside my origins, I am embracing more of the fullness of humanity. I have decided that the best descriptor for who I am vocationally is "an artist of ideas."

In July 2007, I was in South Africa with a group from Bethel University listening to theologian Russell Botman speak at the University of Stellenbosch. He had recently been named the first black rector of the historically white Afrikaner institution. It was eerie and at the same time profoundly emotive to sit and listen to this activist against apartheid discuss his present struggle to transform an institution that gave birth to apartheid. Professor Botman proclaimed that his one motive and primary purpose in pursuing reconciliation was "in the interest of future generations." He then added, "If we do not get it right, future generations will judge this a missed opportunity as they will carry the burden." As I approached and then surpassed the age of fifty, I noticed that my motivation and purpose has shifted to that of Rector Botman. So while this book is a self-expression of my homecoming journey, ultimately I hope it will be a gift to those in the next generation seeking a more reconciled world.

Acknowledgments

The stories in this book already offer an acknowledgement to many who have enriched my journey during the first fifty years of my life. The insights and life of the late Howard Thurman have offered me a particular insight into understanding my journey. This is probably obvious, since often he is the only one whose writings are quoted in a chapter. I want to add a special thank-you to those who took time to read through the manuscript and offer comments: Jonathan DeYoung, Karen DeYoung, Rachel DeYoung, Joseph Donnelly, Mark Horst, Bill Huff, Claudia May, Chris McNair, Sally Messner, Aldean Miles, Mercy Olson Ward, Chris Rice, Gregg Ward, and Cecilia Williams. My sincerest gratitude to Josh Messner for his excellent editorial and design work that moved this from manuscript to published book. And thanks to Bill Huff for never giving up on this project and helping me find a way to get it done.

While on my "homecoming journey" I have lived in a home full of unconditional love. I express my gratitude to Karen, Rachel, and Jonathan for their support.

NOTES

Prologue

The conference in South Africa was sponsored by Youth for Christ. I was invited to speak at this conference by Sean Moodley and Alroy Trout. I had met them the previous year at the Salzburg Seminar (see chapter 5). The worship leader who so skillfully wove together the different languages and cultural styles was Seth Naicker.

1. Howard Thurman, *The Negro Spiritual Speaks of Life and Death* (New York: Harper, 1947), 32.

1. Glimpses of My Humanity in Harlem

I was a youth pastor at the Church of God in Otsego, Michigan. The story from Kansas City, Kansas, occurred in 1999 when I was in the city to share with leaders and community residents what we were learning in Minneapolis and St. Paul about networking for urban change.

1. Story originally told in Curtiss Paul DeYoung, *Coming Together: The Bible's Message in an Age of Diversity* (Valley Forge: Judson, 1995), 172.

2. Howard Thurman, *This Luminous Darkness: A Personal Interpretation of the Anatomy of Segregation and the Ground of Hope* (New York: Harper, 1965), 94.

2. Linked to a Lineage of Mentors

Portions of this chapter were first composed for class papers in my doctoral program at the University of St. Thomas, St. Paul, Minnesota.

1. Curtiss Paul DeYoung, *Reconciliation: Our Greatest Challenge, Our Only Hope* (Valley Forge: Judson, 1997), v.

2. Cain Hope Felder, *Troubling Biblical Waters: Race, Class and Family* (Maryknoll: Orbis, 1989).

3. Cain Hope Felder, ed., *The Original African Heritage Study Bible* (Nashville: James Winston, 1993).

4. Samuel George Hines, "God's One-Item Agenda: The Central Focus of God's Word and Work" in Samuel George Hines and Curtiss

Paul DeYoung, *Beyond Rhetoric: Reconciliation as a Way of Life* (Valley Forge: Judson, 2000), 24–33.

5. Howard Thurman, *Disciplines of the Spirit* (New York: Harper, 1963), 126.

6. Laurent A. Parks Daloz, Cheryl H. Keen, James P. Keen, and Sharon Daloz Parks, *Common Fire: Leading Lives of Commitment in a Complex World* (Boston: Beacon, 1996), 99. The idea that we are linked to a lineage of mentors was an insight I had when reading *Common Fire*. A chapter on mentors notes Mary McLeod Bethune's mentorship of Howard Thurman and others. The authors also mention that Sojourner Truth inspired Bethune.

7. James Earl Massey, "Our Task as Reconcilers," DeYoung Decade Service, TURN —Twin Cities Urban Reconciliation Network, Park Avenue United Methodist Church, Minneapolis, Minnesota, November 4, 2001. Quote taken from audio tape of event.

8. James Earl Massey, *Aspects of my Pilgrimage: An Autobiography* (Anderson: Anderson University Press, 2002), 269.

3. A "White" Malcolm X

1. Cain Hope Felder, "Foreword," in DeYoung, *Coming Together*, x.

2. Story originally told in DeYoung, *Reconciliation*, 118–19.

3. Story originally told in DeYoung, *Reconciliation*, 79–80.

4. Curtiss Paul DeYoung. Michael O. Emerson, George Yancey, and Karen Chai Kim, *United by Faith: The Multiracial Congregation as an Answer to the Problem of Race* (New York: Oxford University Press, 2003).

5. Curtiss Paul DeYoung, *Living Faith: How Faith Inspires Social Justice* (Minneapolis: Fortress, 2007).

4. Taco Bell Lutheran

Portions of the section on First Church of God were first prepared for a doctoral course at the University of St. Thomas. The alternative Sunday School class at First Church of God was designed and taught by Robert Odom. The woman who brought the first Hmong youngster to First Church of God was the late Laura Thompson.

TURN had many excellent staff people during my ten years. I am particularly grateful to Pat Peterson, Robin Bell, and Terry Coffee who served as vice presidents and Sheila Ford, Dawn Corlew, Joy Skjegstad, and Anne Oliver as program directors. The board chairpersons during my tenure at TURN were Terry Coffee, Peggy Jones, Kim Vu Friesen, Gary Downing, and Karen McKinney. TURN operated its programs with many partners including The McKnight Foundation, Wallestad Foundation, St. Paul Area Council of Churches, Greater Minneapolis Council of Churches, Jewish Relations Council, Masjid An-Nur, World Vision, Hennepin County, University of St. Thomas, Stairstep Initiative, and several congregations and faith-based nonprofit organizations. Key partners in the Hawthorne-Jordan Ministerial Alliance were the General Mills Foundation and the Northwest Area Foundation.

Interlude One—Roots in Roxbury

1. Ethel Stanwood Bolton, compiler, *Immigrants to New England, 1700–1775* (Clearfield Company, 1931, 2004), 41. Bolton notes in the preface to the book, "In some cases, mostly in the records of ships entering Boston, those may have been included as immigrants who were merely returning from a trip to New York, or even abroad." This was likely the case of the Bedoonas.

2. Francis S. Drake, *The Town of Roxbury: Memorable Persons and Places* (Boston: Municipal Printing Office, 1908), 341. Other sources of information on the Crafts family come from James M. Crafts and William F. Crafts, *The Crafts Family: A Genealogical and Biographical History of the Descendants of Griffin and Alice Craft of Roxbury, Mass., 1630–1890* (Northhampton: Gazette, 1893).

3. *A Report of the Record Commissioners of the City of Boston, Containing Boston Marriages from 1700 to 1751* (Boston: Municipal Printing Office, 1898), 7.

4. Lorenzo Johnston Greene, *The Negro in Colonial New England* (New York: Atheneum, 1942, 1974), 50–51; A. Leon Higginbotham Jr., *In the Matter of Color: Race and the American Legal Process—The Colonial Period*, (New York: Oxford University Press, 1978), 61.

5. Photocopy of Administration of Thomas Beduna, Roxbury, Mass., Probate Index 1636–1894, No. 6428, filed by Hon. Josiah Willard Esq., Boston, April 23, 1734, "An inventory of the Estate of Thomas Beduna at Roxbury who died the 31 of March 1733." He owned one house and barn, eight acres of land, as well as orchards, plowing, pasture, cows, and so on. His wife Lydia was still alive and presented the inventory of her late husband who was a husbandman.

6. Greene, 16, 126.

7. Robert C. Twombley and Robert H. Moore, "Black Puritan: The Negro in Seventeenth-Century Massachusetts," in Bruce A. Glasrud and Alan M. Smith, editors, *Race Relations in British North America, 1607-1783* (Chicago: Nelson-Hall, 1982), 146.

8. Greene, 339.

9. Twombley and Moore, 147.

10. Twombley and Moore, 156.

11. Kevin Mumford, "After Hugh: Statutory Race Segregation in Colonial America, 1630–1725," *The American Journal of Legal History* 43/3 (July 1999): 285, 293; Twombley and Moore, 156.

12. Greene, 126.

13. Mumford, 294.

14. Crafts and Crafts, 46; Walter Eliot Thwing, *History of the First Church in Roxbury Massachusetts, 1630–1904* (Boston: Butterfield, 1908), 135.

5. A Global Faith

Portions of this chapter first appeared in Curtiss Paul DeYoung, "Fellows' Commentary on Session 372—Curtiss Paul DeYoung." *A Record of Session 372—Race and Ethnicity: Social Change through Public Awareness, October 9–16, 1999—Salzburg Seminar* (Salzburg Seminar Staff, ed.). Salzburg, Austria: Salzburg Seminar, 2000.

1. Curtiss Paul DeYoung, *Milwaukee's Faith Community Speaks* (Milwaukee: Social Development Commission, 1991).

6. The Jesus Was Black Tour

My first visit to South Africa was at the invitation of Sean Moodley and Alroy Trout. As of this writing, I have visited South Africa on ten occasions. The first two visits were at the invitation of Youth for Christ—Johannesburg. The Jesus Was Black Tour in 2003 was a sizeable undertaking. The key organizers in Johannesburg were Sean Moodley, Alroy Trout, Seth and Merrishia Naicker, and David and Joyce Naicker. In Cape Town, Eddie Jacobs and Anthony Meyer, of the singing group the Christian Explainers, coordinated my itinerary. Also Njabulo and Mpho Ndebele, Brendon and Gaylene Adams, and Alan Jansen added extremely meaningful moments to my schedule. In Port Elizabeth, Philile Lobese hosted me. In Durban, Craig Bouchier organized my time.

The Jesus Was Black Tour was coordinated under the auspices of the City Gate Project in Minneapolis, Minnesota (where I was the executive director). Seven organizations were sponsors: Bethel University, St. Paul, Minnesota; Biblical Institute for Social Change, Washington, DC (Dr. Cain Hope Felder, president); First Church of God, Columbus, Ohio (Bishop Timothy Clarke, senior pastor); Mount Olivet Missionary Baptist Church, St. Paul, Minnesota (Rev. James Thomas, senior pastor); National Association of the Church of God, West Middlesex, Pennsylvania (Dr. Tyrone

Cushman, general overseer); Park Avenue United Methodist Church, Minneapolis, Minnesota (Dr. Mark Horst, senior pastor); and Trinity United Church of Christ, Chicago, Illinois (Dr. Jeremiah Wright Jr., senior pastor).

1. Howard Thurman, *Jesus and the Disinherited* (New York: Abingdon-Cokesbury, 1949), 11, 13.

7. The Peace of Jerusalem

The key persons who coordinated the schedule for my trips to Palestine and Israel were Allyn Dhynes (World Vision—Jerusalem), Timothy Seidel (Mennonite Central Committee—Bethlehem), and Eliyahu McLean (Jerusalem Peacemakers). Kathy Kamphoefner of American Friends Service Committee organized my visit to Bi'lin.

1. Elias Chacour, *Blood Brothers* (Grand Rapids: Chosen, 1984, 2003).

Interlude Two—Roots in Africa

1. Greene, 32.

2. This information was retrieved from: http://www.geocities.com/pieterderideaux/idris_notes.html on 9/11/2007 and http://www.geocities.com/pieterderideaux/marino_sanudo.html on 8/9/2007.

Epilogue—The Homecoming Dance

1. DeYoung, *Reconciliation*, 113–14.

2. Howard Thurman, *Meditations for Apostles of Sensitiveness* (Mills College: Eucalyptus, 1948), 1.

Afterword—The Journey Continues

1. Frank Madison Reid III, "Jesus Had an African Connection," Bethel African Methodist Episcopal Church, Baltimore, Maryland, December 1, 1996. Quote taken from video tape.

2. DeYoung, *Milwaukee's Faith Community Speaks*.

3. Curtiss Paul DeYoung, Wilda C. Gafney, Leticia Guardiola-Saenz, George "Tink" Tinker, and Frank M. Yamada, eds., *The Peoples' Bible, New Revised Standard Version with Apocrypha* (Minneapolis: Fortress, 2008).

4. Marcus J. Borg, *The Heart of Christianity; Rediscovering a Life of Faith* (San Francisco: Harper SanFrancisco, 2003), 155–56.